Published by Aperitifs Publishing Company
Santa Rosa, California

Copyright: December 2023
Revised Edition: April 2024

Compiled & Published by John C. Burton, Steve & Christie Curtiss
johncburton@msn.com
707-523-1611

ISBN: 9781732453081
Library of Congress Number: 2023923472

Printed in the United States of America

All rights reserved. No part of this book may be reproduced or transformed in any form or by any means, electronic or mechanical, including photocopying, recording or by any information storage and/or retrieval system without permission in writing from the publisher.

FRONT COVER ACKNOWLEDGEMENTS

GLOBE MINERAL WATER S. F.	Steve & Christie Curtiss Collection
T & H SONOMA. CAL.	John C. Burton Collection
PHILLIPS SODA WATER S. F.	Steve & Christie Curtiss Collection
EL DORADO BOTTLING CO.	Steve & Christie Curtiss Collection
ROYAL SODA WATER WORKS S. F.	Steve & Christie Curtiss Collection
PEERLESS GINGER ALE CO. S. F.	Steve & Christie Curtiss Collection

REAR COVER ACKNOWLEDGEMENTS

C. F. RILEY	John Louder Collection
PEARSON BROS. BODIE	Steve & Christie Curtiss Collection
GOLDEN WEST SODA WORKS MOUNTAIN VIEW	Steve & Christie Curtiss Collection
BOWLAND & CRAIG CITY PHARMACY SAN BERNADINO	Eddie Kuskie Collection

SPECIAL APPRECIATION TO

Special appreciation to Peck & Audie Markota's daughter Jeanne Deschamps and granddaughter Julie Youngblood for allowing us to reference and reprint with updates and additions, *CALIFORNIA HUTCHINSON TYPE SODA BOTTLES* originally printed in 1999. That book is our inspiration. Without their family's permission a portion of bottle collecting history would slowly fade.

Acknowledgements

Where do I start? First of course is the appreciation of Peck & Audie Markota for all the information they brought to us collectors especially considering they didn't have the advantage of today's computers, on-line availability including California Digital Newspapers.
I completely and totally respect their endeavors.

Steve & Christie Curtiss. Without them the majority of this book would be totally incomplete. I made a "cold call" to them suggested by Mike Southworth, not knowing what to expect. I was greeted with open arms. They have an amazing collection of California gravitating stoppers, hutch, and crown top bottles. Their collection is as large as their kindness and heart. I'm forever thankful to them both.

Eddie Kuskie. Again, a "cold call" to a legend I've heard about through the years and his response was positive immediately, sending me photos of bottles I'd never knew existed. His immediate response gave me confidence that this book would go forward and be completed.

Bob & Arlene Hansen. Again a "cold call" and welcomed with open arms by a couple who have an amazing collection of Humboldt County bottles. Well, not just Humboldt County bottles as Bob has the largest collection of Colorado whiskey jugs ever assembled. Thanks to both of them for their hospitality.

Dale Chase, Northwestern Bottle Collector's Association Santa Rosa, Ca. member who assisted in the filming of bottles at Steve & Christie's home. John Louder, who supplied the image of Ed Henry Napa hutch & the outstanding cobalt Eureka Riley's hutch.

Jay Kasper who supplied the image of the unique San Francisco Hercules hutch. Greatly appreciated.

James Quinn. I met James at the Auburn 2023 bottle show and immediately struck up a conversation regarding this book. His response by immediately sending photos of missing bottles is greatly appreciated. In addition, seeing a young person his age who is enthusiastic and as knowledgeable as he is gives me faith that the future of the hobby is in good hands.

Jeff Wichmann, American Bottle Auctions, who always allows me to use photos of rare images in my books. Brent Henningsen for the Salinas Steigelman bottle.

Mike Southworth who suggested this endeavor & Brent Henningsen for the Monterey Hutch image. And recently discovered valuable information on the HutchBook.com URL site.

I've learned by assembling this book that bottle collectors willingly open their doors to one that is trying to preserve the history of our hobby and collections. I also found that those that I didn't know and "cold called" are the friendliest, possibly because we're not in competition with each other locally at estate sales, flea markets, garage sales and antique stores.

From what I've seen doing this book; we can't have it all. JB

ADDITIONAL PUBLICATIONS BY JOHN C. BURTON
Aperitifs Publishing Santa Rosa, Ca.

Grace Bros. Breweries, History & Memorabilia
Santa Rosa – Los Angeles – Sacramento – Fresno

Bottles, Tokens, & History of Sonoma County
Soda, Beer, and Whiskey Bottles Featuring Saloon Tokens
Contributions By Merle Avila, John Louder, Richard Siri, Rick Siri & Dan Brown

Lake, Napa, Sonoma, Mendocino, Solano, Marin & Humboldt Mineral & Hot Springs
John C. Burton & John Louder

San Rafael – Sausalito – San Anselmo Soda, Seltzer, Beer, and Spirits Bottles
A Guide and Reference to Bottlers of Beer, Soda, Seltzer,
and Spirits of Marin County including a listing of Antique Bottles

Bob Welch Collection of California
Pre-Prohibition, Prohibition and California
Permit & IRTP Paper Label Bottles and labels

Sonoma County Pharmacy, Proprietary & Drug Store Bottles
Featuring Bottles, Advertising and Dose Glasses
Co-Author Frank Sternad

Splits & That's It
A Guide and To California Pre-Prohibition Half Pint Beer Bottles
Blob Tops, Baltimore Loop & Crown Top Bottles
Mike Burgess Collection

Western Beers
Tim Higgins Manuscript
Compiled & Reprinted By John C. Burton

Early Soda, Mineral Water Bottles of The Old West
An Updated Reprint of Peck & Audie Markota's Book
Compiled & Reprinted By John C. Burton

Early Medicine Bottles of The Western Frontier
Tim Higgins Manuscript
Compiled & Reprinted By John C. Burton

ALAMEDA

ALAMEDA SODA WATER CO. ALAMEDA, CAL.

Face: #1   ALAMEDA
Circa 1898 - 1902   (Hands shaking)
                              SODA WATER CO.
                              OAKLAND, CAL.
                              BOTTLE IS NOT TO BE SOLD

Face: #2 & 3   ALAMEDA
Circa 1902-1919   (Hands shaking)
                              SODA WATER CO.
                              BOTTLE IS NOT TO BE SOLD

Face: #4   ALAMEDA
Circa 1902 - 1919   (Hands shaking)
                              SODA WATER CO.

Reverse:	Blank
Bottom:	Some have numbers
Color:	Aqua, light green & lime
Circa:	1898 – 1919
Locality:	Alameda Cal. Alameda County
Rarity:	#1 Ex. Rare – Others scarce
Value(s)	$_____ $_____
	$_____ $_____
Markota	Pages 3-4

Founded by Thomas Lund & Lot Moore in 1898 located at 2303 Buena Vista Avenue, Alameda. Moore left in 1900 and Lund relocated the business to 622 Harrison Street in Oakland with Isaac H. Spiro President and Lawrence J. Spiro Vice President eventually moving to 802 East 12th Street.

Left John Burton Collection
Right Steve & Christie Curtiss Collection

Face number 4

ALAMEDA
EMPIRE SODA WORKS

Face:	EMPIRE SODA WORKS
	WEISS & Co.
Reverse:	Blank
Bottom:	Blank
Color:	Aqua
Circa:	1883 – 1887
Locality:	Alameda, Cal. Alameda County
Rarity:	
Value:	$_____
Markota:	Page 41

Moritz Weiss a former brewer for pacific Brewery of San Francisco & George Siegler a brewer from Alameda started the Empire Soda Works in Alameda on Blanding Avenue between Oak & Park & Streets.

In 1884 Siegler went to work at the Oakland Brewery and George Lehmann became Weiss's new partner until 1887.

They sold to Edward Schaad & Conrad Schafer who changed the name to Alameda Empire Soda Works. Schaad & Schafer lasted one year closing in 1889.

Steve & Christie Curtiss Collection

ALAMEDA

	EMPIRE SODA WORKS
Face:	EMPIRE SODA WORKS
	ALAMEDA
	CAL.
Reverse:	Blank
Bottom:	Blank
Color:	Aqua
Circa:	1889 – 1892
Locality:	Alameda, Cal. Alameda County
Rarity:	Common
Value:	$_____
Markota:	Page 40

George F. Taylor reopened the Empire Soda works in 1889 on the north corner of Clements & Oak Streets.

Steve & Christie Curtiss Collection

ALAMEDA

EMPIRE SODA WORKS

Face: EMPIRE SODA WORKS
         ALAMEDA
Reverse: Blank
Bottom: Blank
Color: Aqua
Circa: 1889 – 1892
Locality: Alameda, Cal. Alameda County
Rarity: Common
Value: $_____
Markota: Page 40

In 1892 Jules Somps & Jean Meillette became the new owners moving to 2301 Buena Vista Avenue closing in 1895

Left - John Burton Collection
Right – Steve & Christie Curtiss Collection

ALTURAS

ALTURAS SODA WORKS

Face: ALTURAS
         SODA WORKS
         ALTURAS
         CAL.
Reverse: Blank
Bottom: Blank
Color: Aqua
Circa: 1880 – 1890
Locality: Alturas, Cal.
Rarity: Extremely Rare
Value: $_____
Markota: Page 4

W. B. McCollum & Company were listed as proprietors.

Steve & Christie Curtiss Collection

AMADOR

AMADOR COUNTY SODA WORKS

Face: AMADOR COUNTY
SODA WORKS

Reverse: Blank
Bottom: GRAVITATING STOPPER MADE BY JOHN MATTHEWS PAT. OCT. 11, 1864 NEW YORK
Color: Aqua
Circa: 1879 -1891
Locality: Jackson, Cal.
Rarity: Semi Common
Value: $_____
Markota: Page 5

Started by George W. Russ & Henry Carsten In the mid 1870's Jackson. Russ left in 1886 going to Santa Rosa Soda Works. Carstens operated the business until the early 1890's selling to T. K. Norman, and moving to Modesto joining up with George Russ who had left Santa Rosa purchasing the Stanislaus Soda Works as partners until 1893.

John Burton Collection

ANGEL'S CAMP

ANGEL'S BREWERY AND SODA WORKS

Face: ANGEL'S BREWERY
AND
SODA WORKS
E. F. HUBLER
PROP.

Reverse: Blank
Bottom: Blank
Color: Aqua
Circa: 1893 – 1912
Locality: Angels Camp, Cal.
Rarity: Scarce
Value: $_____
Markota: Page 6

Ernest F. Hubler operated the brewery & soda works from 1893 until 1912 when A. D. Mentz purchased the business and more than likely went to crown top bottles.

John Burton Collection

ANGEL'S CAMP

SEQUOIA SODA WORKS

Face:	SEQUOIA
	SODA WORKS
	ANGELS
	CAL.

Reverse:	Blank
Bottom:	Blank
Color:	Aqua
Circa:	1905 - 1920
Location:	Angels Camp, Cal.
Rarity:	Extremely Rare
Value:	$_____
Markota:	Page 125

Not sure of this hutch listed in Markota book because if Banchers started in 1905 he would have started with crown tops as hutches were on their way out

Nate Banchers was listed as proprietor from 1905 to 1912. In 1913 Louis A. Deveggio purchased the bottling company until 1920 more than likely using crown top bottles.

ANTIOCH

PIONEER SODA WORKS

Face:	PIONEER
	SODA WORKS
	ANTIOCH

Reverse:	Blank
Bottom:	Blank
Color:	Aqua
Circa:	1880 - 1900
**Locality:	Antioch, Cal.
Rarity:	Rare**
Value:	$_____
**Markota:	Page 103**

In 1880 John Gagen founded Pioneer Soda Works in Antioch manufacturing ginger ale, sarsaparilla, & cider. Around 1900 the business became the Antioch Soda Works.

Steve & Christie Curtiss Collection

ARCATA

	ARCATA SODA WORKS
Face:	ARCATA
	B. P.
	SODA WORKS
Reverse:	Blank
Bottom:	Blank
Color:	Aqua
Circa:	1886 – 1896
Locality:	Arcata, Cal. (Humboldt County)
Rarity:	Very Rare
Value:	$_____
Markota:	Page 6

Bartholomew Pouleur established Arcata Soda Works in 1886 in Humboldt County when Arcata was known as Union Town.

Bartholomew died August 12, 1893 and his son-in-law John Balance Sammons managed the business until October 1893, leasing to Thomas Tierney & John Morrison who operated it until September 1894. A second son-in-law, Edward Ellis operated it until July 1895 when Bartholomew's son Jules managed it under the name Arcata Bottling Works until June 1896.

John Burton Collection

AUBURN

	J. & R. BOTTLING WORKS
Face:	J & R
	AUBURN
Reverse:	Blank
Bottom:	Blank
Color:	Aqua
Circa:	1885 – 1889
Locality:	Auburn
Rarity:	Rare
Value:	$_____
Markota:	Page 66

Conrad Johnson and Jacob Bull were proprietors of the Johnson & Roll Bottling Works. Albert Kenison joined the firm becoming the Roll & Kenison company.

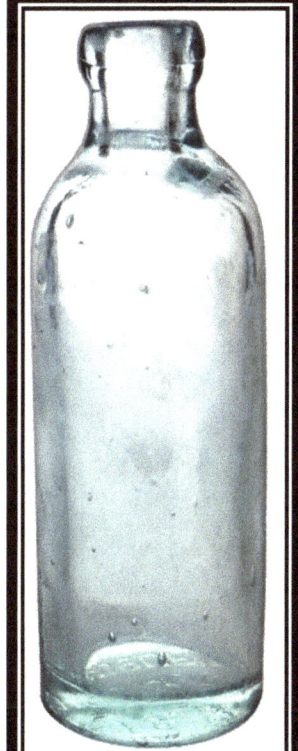

John Burton Collection

AUBURN

A.W. K. AUBURN, CAL.

Face:	Blank - Paper label?
Reverse:	Blank
Bottom:	A.W.K.& Co.
	AUBURN
	CAL.
Color:	Aqua
Circa:	1901- 1910 (Hutch bottles)
Locality:	Auburn, Cal.
Rarity:	Common
Value:	$_____
Markota:	Page 8

Albert Wesley Kenison took over the company in 1901 from Jacob Roll & Conrad Johnson. Kenison died in 1904 of blood poisoning and plant manager Walter Jacobs continued the business until 1943 with his son's James and Robert continuing the business until 1950

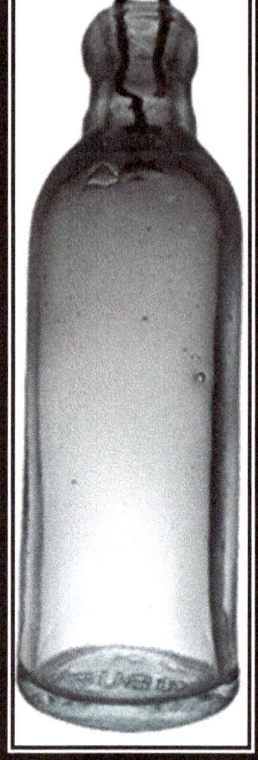

Eddie Kuskie Collection

BAKERSFIELD

HENRY CONDICT BAKERSFIELD SODA WORKS

Face:	H. F. CONDICT
	BAKERSFIELD
Variant:	Marble top stopper type bottle
Reverse:	Blank
Bottom:	Blank
Color:	Aqua
Circa:	1880 - 1920
Locality:	Bakersfield
Value:	$_____
Markota:	Page 31

In 1880 Henry Condict started the Bakersfield Soda Works on G Street between 17th & 18th. He went to crown top bottles like most bottlers around 1910.

Steve & Christie Curtiss Collection

BAKERSFIELD – SUMNER

SUMNER & BAKERSFIELD SODA WORKS

Face: G. GALLI
SODA WORKS
SUMNER
&
BAKERSFIELD
Reverse: Blank
Bottom: G
Color: Aqua
Circa: 1888 - 1904
Locality: Sumner becoming Kern City
Rarity: Rare
Value: $_____
Markota: Page 49

Giacomi Galli established the soda works on Grove Street in Bakersfield then Southern Pacific split the area and in 1893 an area northeast became known as Sumner also known as Kern City. In 1909 Kern City & Bakersfield voted to became one city; Bakersfield.

Steve & Christie Curtiss Collection

BELMONT

BELMONT SODA WORKS

Face: BELMONT
SODA WORKS
Vertical: Trade Horseshoe Mark
CAL.
Reverse: Blank
Bottom: Blank
Color: Aqua
Circa: 1880 – 1900
Locality: Belmont, Cal.
Rarity: Rare
Value: $_____
Markota: Page 14

J. F. Janke started the Belmont Soda Works in the early 1880's and also operated the Belmont Picnic Grounds until 1900.

Steve & Christie Curtiss Collection

BENICIA

BENICIA STEAM SODA WORKS

Face: BENICIA
             STEAM
             SODA WORKS
             GUSTAV GNAUCK

Reverse: Blank
Bottom: Blank
Color: Aqua
Circa: 1907 – 1915
Locality: Benicia, Cal.
Value: $_____
Markota: Page 14

John Massle & Gustav Gnuack purchased the Benicia Brewery early 1880's on the corner of First & H Streets from John Rueger. In 1886 Gnauck became sole owner and after the 1906 earthquake started bottling soda for the mass of people that moved to Benicia from San Francisco.

BERKELEY

GILBERT HALL SODA WORKS

Face: GILBERT HALL
             BERKELEY
             CAL.

Reverse: Blank
Bottom: <25>
Color: Aqua
Circa: 1892 -1894
Locality: Berkeley
Rarity: Extremely Rare
Value: $_____
Markota: Page 56

Gilbert Hall removed Agers from the partnership and operated the Berkeley Soda Works closing in two years.

Agers who was working as a horseshoer convinced John J. Koughan to become his partner and reopened the Berkeley Soda Works again for another short stint.

John Burton Collection

Steve & Christie Curtiss Collection

BERKELEY

R. L. AGERS SODA WORKS

Face:	R. L. AGERS
	& Co.
Monogram:	A C
	BERKELEY, CAL.
Base:	10 - Sided panel
Variant:	Without Slug Plate
Reverse:	Blank
Bottom:	Some have large dot
Circa:	1889 – 1901
Locality:	Berkeley
Rarity:	Scarce
Value:	$_____
Markota:	Page 3

Located on corner of Dwight Way & Telegraph Avenue. Relocated to Dwight Way & Humboldt Street in 1889 taking Herman Cory as partner.

1891 Agers relocated back to Dwight Way & Telegraph Streets with new partner Gilbert Hall.

1892 Agers was gone and now Hall as proprietor. 1894 business closed. 1895 Agers returned with new partner John J. Koughan lasting until 1896. The business closed forever.

Steve & Christie Curtiss Collection

BERKELEY

BERKELEY SODA WORKS

Face:	BERKELEY SODA
	WORKS
	A & K
	BERKELEY
	CAL.
Base:	10- Sided panel
Reverse:	Blank
Bottom:	A & K
Color:	Aqua
Circa:	1895 – 1896
Locality:	Berkeley
Rarity:	Extremely Rare
Value:	$_____
Markota:	Page 14

When Gilbert Hall closed the soda works in 1894 Agers returned in 1895 with John J. Koughan the partnership lasting until 1896.

Steve & Christie Curtiss Collection

BERKELEY

ARTIC SODA WATER COMPANY

Face: ARTIC
SODA WATER Co.
BERKELEY
CAL.
Reverse: Blank
Bottom: A
Color: Aqua
Locality: Berkeley, Cal.
Circa: 1893 – 1903
Rarity: Rare
Value: $_____
Markota: Page

E. Mayeo & Joseph Kelly operated the Artic Soda Water Company at 2505 Telegraph Avenue starting in 1898 when Mayeo left in 1899.

George Mayle & Joseph Kelly's partnership lasted one year and in 1900 Robert L. Agers, former owner of Berkeley Soda Works purchased the Artic Soda Water Company closing the business in 1903.

John Burton Collection

BLACK DIAMOND

BLACK DIAMOND ^1 SODA WORKS

Face: BLACK DIAMOND
^1
SODA WORKS
Reverse: Blank
Bottom: Blank
Color: Aqua
Circa: 1880 – 1894
Location: Black Diamond, Cal.
Rarity: Semi Common
Value: $_____
Markota: Page 16

Left - John Burton Collection
Right – Steve & Christie Curtiss Collection

BISHOP

       T. SHONE BOTTLING WORKS
Face: T. SHONE
Reverse: Blank
Bottom: Blank
Color: Aqua
Circa: 1880 – 1894
Location: Bishop, Cal.
Rarity: Semi Rare
Value: $_____
Markota: Page 126

John Burton Collection

BISHOP

       INYO SODA WORKS
Face: INYO SODA WORKS
                 BISHOP CAL.
Reverse: Blank
Bottom: Blank
Color: Aqua
Circa: 1899 - 1908
Locality: Bishop, Cal.
Rarity: Extremely Rare
Value: $_____
Markota: Page 65

In 1889 C. E. Johnson was proprietor of Inyo Soda Works on Grove Street near Main. He bottled all flavors but mainly root beer which sold for five cents a bottle or .75 cents a case. He sold to Leichman & Stout in 1908 who changed the name to Inyo Bottling Works and relocated to Hammond Street.

Steve & Christie Curtiss Collection

BODIE

PEARSON BROTHERS
Face:	PEARSON BROS. BODIE
Reverse:	Blank
Bottom:	Blank
Color:	Both Aqua & Teal
Circa:	1882 – 1891
Locality:	Bodie, Cal.
Rarity:	Extremely Rare
Value:	$_____
Markota:	Page 100

Local dealer Mr. Brodigan was bought out by the Pearson Brothers of Placerville who then developed a water system from Rough Creek and from a spring at Lowe Street. The water was bottled in Bodie from the spring and diverted water from Rough Creek to a reservoir.

Pearson brothers were experienced in the soda business having had a soda works in Placerville since 1852.

Steve & Christie Curtiss Collection

CHICO

A. F. BLOOD SODA WORKS
Face:	Blank
Reverse:	Blank
Bottom:	A. F. BLOOD CHICO CAL.
Color:	Aqua
Circa:	1870 – 1884
Locality:	Chico, Cal.
Rarity:	Rare
Value:	$_____
Markota:	Page 17

Amos Blood started the soda works at 7th and Broadway. In 1884 he had $20 in working capital and was $1,500 in debt.

He sold to A. G. Eames in 1895 who also was in the ice business and handled mineral water, wholesaled beer, and soda water.

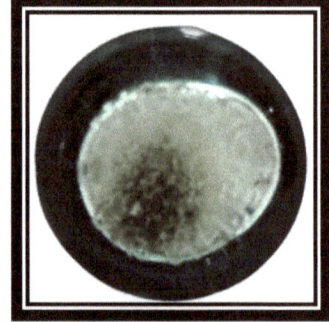

Steve & Christie Curtiss Collection

CHICO

	CHICO SODA WORKS
Face:	CHICO
	SODA WORKS
Reverse:	Blank
Bottom:	C S W
Color:	Clear, Lime green & Sun color
Circa:	1885 – 1930
Locality:	Chico, Cal.
Rarity:	Lime green rare others common
Value:	$_____ Lime Green
	$_____ Others
Markota:	Page 28

Eames build a new soda works plant on the corner of Fifth & Ivy Streets in 1895 continuing until 1930 when bought out by Seven-Up Company.

COLUSA

	COLUSA SODA WORKS
Face:	COLUSA
	SODA WORKS
	COLUSA
	CAL.
Reverse:	Blank
Bottom:	Some have 328 H
Base:	306 H
Circa:	1877 – 1910
Locality:	Colusa, Cal.
Rarity:	Extremely Rare
Value:	$_____
Markota:	Page 30

Started in 1877 by J. L. Poulson & Brower at the corner of 3rd & Market Streets. In 1878 Brower was out and H. Eller was a partner. Fire destroyed the building in 1878 reopening in 1879 with Eller out and T. H. Polly a new partner.

Paulson retired in 1885 and Polly took on Rankin Blackburn as a partner in 1887. Blackburn became sole owner a year later and sold to T. F. Phillips in 1900 who operated the business at least until 1910.

John Burton Collection

 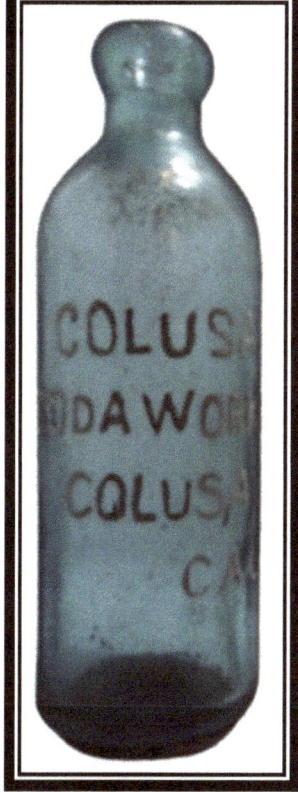

Steve & Christie Curtiss Collection

COLUSA

          COLUSA SODA WORKS
Face: J. W. DAVIS
                COLUSA, CAL.
Reverse: Blank
Bottom: Blank
Base:
Circa:
Locality: Colusa, Cal.
Rarity: Extremely Rare
Value: $_____
Markota: Unlisted

Steve & Christie Curtiss Collection

CROCKETT

          CROCKETT SODA WORKS
Face: CROCKETT
                Star monogram
                SODA WORKS
Reverse: Blank
Bottom: Blank
Color: Aqua
Circa: 1895 - 1905
Locality: Crockett, Cal.
Rarity: Extremely Rare
Value: $_____
Markota: Page 32

Late 1880's Beda & Company were listed as owners. Beda also owned the Star Hotel and that gives speculation to the reason there is a star on the bottle.

Steve & Christie Curtiss Collection

DIXON

	DIXON SODA WORKS
Face:	DIXON SODA WORKS
Reverse:	Blank
Bottom:	Some plain or S & O or K
Color:	Aqua
Circa:	1883 – 1918
Locality:	Dixon, Cal.
Rarity:	Scarce
Value:	$_____
Markota:	Page 37

Established by Frank Kane in 1883 on First near Main Street. Kane sold to Hans Schomer &and Albert Oberholzer in 1888. They were also agents for Tolenas Mineral Springs water. Oberholzer left the company around 1905 leaving Schomer as sole owner until 1918.

Steve & Christie Curtiss Collection

EL DORADO

	EL DORADO BOTTLING CO.
Face:	EL DORADO BOTTLING CO.
Reverse:	Blank
Bottom:	Blank
Color:	Aqua
Circa:	1890's
Locality:	El Dorado, Cal.
Rarity:	Extremely rare
Value:	$_____
Markota:	Unlisted

Steve & Christie Curtiss Collection

EEL RIVER VALLEY (SPRINGVILLE)
EEL RIVER VALLEY SODA WORKS

Face:	EEL RIVER VALLEY SODA WORKS SPRINGVILLE, CAL.
Reverse:	Blank
Bottom:	328 H
Color:	Aqua
Circa:	Late 1880's – 1890's
Location:	Springville, Cal.
Rarity:	Extremely Rare
Value:	$ _____
Markota:	Page 38

Operated by Joseph Monroe. Springville was the name of the old area of Fortuna & Rohnerville.

John Burton Collection

EEL RIVER VALLEY (SPRINGVILLE)
EEL RIVER VALLEY SODA WORKS

Face:	EEL RIVER VALLEY SPRINGVILLE CAL. SODA WORKS
Reverse:	Blank
Bottom:	Blank
Circa:	Late 1880's – 1890's
Color:	Aqua
Location:	Springville, Cal.
Rarity:	Extremely Rare
Value:	$ _____
Markota:	Page 38

Operated by John & Charles Monroe. Springville was the name of the old area of Fortuna & Rohnerville. John married into a family with extensive apple orchards and bottled apple cider.

John Burton Collection

EUREKA
J. P. MONROE BOTTLING WORKS

Face:	J. P. MONROE & Co. EUREKA HUMBOLDT Co. CAL.
Reverse:	Blank
Bottom:	GRAVITATING STOPPER MADE BY JOHN MATTHEWS PAT. OCT. 11, 1864 NEW YORK
Color:	Aqua
Circa:	Late 1880's
Location:	Eureka, Cal.
Rarity:	Rare
Value:	$ _____
Markota:	Page 84

This bottle is attributed to both Joseph Sr. and son, Alonso W. Monroe. The soda company was listed at the corner of A & Washington Streets.

Left – Bob & Arlene Hansen Collection
Right – Steve & Christie Curtiss Collection

EUREKA
A. MONROE & CO.

Face:	A. MONROE & Co. EUREKA, H. C. CAL.
Reverse:	Blank
Bottom:	GRAVITATING STOPPER MADE BY JOHN MATTHEWS PAT. OCT. 11, 1864 NEW YORK
Circa:	February 23, 1876
Location:	Eureka, Cal.
Rarity:	Scarce
Value:	$ _____
Markota:	Page 82

Located at 5th & A streets in Eureka Alonzo Monroe established the Humboldt Soda Works & Brewing Company and was the patriarch of the Monroe family and had bottling plants in Eureka, Ferndale and Fortuna. In 1887 John started his own bottling plant in Springville (Fortuna). Later A younger brother, Charles joined John.

Left - Bob & Arlene Hansen Collection
Right – Steve & Christie Curtiss Collection

EUREKA
HUCK (or HOLBERT) & JOSEPH P. MONROE

Face:	H & M
	EUREKA
	CAL.
Reverse:	Blank
Bottom:	X
Circa:	Late 1870's - Early 1880's
Color:	Aqua
Location:	Eureka, Cal.
Rarity:	Rare
Value:	$ _____
Markota:	Page 56

Late 1870's Joseph Sr. partnered with Mr. Huck and/or Holbert for a few short years.

John Burton Collection

EUREKA
HUMBOLDT ARTESIAN MINERAL WATER

Face:	HUMBOLDT
	ARTESIAN
	MINERAL WATER
	EUREKA, CAL.
Reverse:	Blank
Bottom:	Blank
Color:	Aqua
Circa:	1890's - 1912
Location:	Eureka, Cal.
Rarity:	Rare
Value:	$ _____
Markota:	Page 64

Located at 227-229 D Street relocating several times and finally in 1900 landing on F Street between Humboldt & Trinity Streets. The final prior move prior to 1912 seems to be to Whipple Street.

Left - John Burton Collection
Right – Bob & Arlene Hansen Collection

EUREKA

MONROE CIDER & VINEGAR COMPANY

Face: MONROE
                        CIDER & VINEGAR Co.
                        EUREKA
                        CAL.

Reverse: Blank
Bottom: Blank
Circa: 1902 - 1910
Location: Eureka, Cal.
Rarity: Scarce
Value: $ _____
Markota: Page 83

John W. Monroe was listed as proprietor of Monroe Cider & Vinegar Company located on the Corner of I & Myrtle Streets in Eureka.

Steve & Christie Curtiss Collection

EUREKA

MONROE DISTILLED SODA WATER

Face: MONROE
                        DISTILLED
                        SODA WATER
                        EUREKA. CAL.

Reverse: Blank
Bottom: Blank
Circa: 1902 - 1910
Location: Eureka, Cal.
Rarity: Scarce
Value: $ _____
Markota: Page 84

Covering all angles of the soda, cider & vinegar business John W. Monroe also bottled distilled water at the I & Myrtle Street plant.

John Burton Collection

EUREKA
CITY EUREKA SODA WORKS

Face:	CITY EUREKA SODA WORKS
Reverse:	Blank
Bottom:	Blank
Color:	Aqua
Circa:	1890 -1915
Location:	Eureka, Cal.
Rarity:	Common
Value:	$ _____
Markota:	Page 29

In competition to Monroe, John O'Dea & John Morrison managed the City Eureka Soda Works and in 1895 O'Dea opened his own soda water company.

Pete Delaney purchased the City Eureka Bottling Works in 1898 moving the plant temporally to 318 F Street in 1902 then to 424 3rd Street. In 1903 Can Young joined Delaney.

In 1906 they were bottling at John O'Dea's factory at 1126 Pine Street.

John Burton Collection

EUREKA
JOHN O'DEA BOTTLING WORKS

Face:	JOHN O'DEA EUREKA CAL. BOTTLING WORKS
Reverse:	Blank
Bottom:	Blank
Color:	Aqua
Circa:	1895 - 1906
Location:	Eureka, Cal.
Rarity:	Semi Rare
Value:	$ _____
Markota:	Page 96

John O'Dea with John Morrison operated the bottling plant at 1126, Pine Street until 1906 when Peter Delaney & Can Young purchased the company.

John Burton Collection

EUREKA

DELANEY & YOUNG SODA WORKS
Face:	**DELANEY & YOUNG**
	EUREKA, CAL.
Reverse:	Blank
Bottom:	Blank
Color:	Aqua
Circa:	1903 - 1914
Location:	Eureka, Cal.
Rarity:	Rare
Value:	$ _____
Markota:	Page 35

Proprietors Peter Delaney & Can Young bottled soda at 318 F Street then moving to 424 Third Street.

A second variation of their bottle does not have "CAL. On the face.

John Burton Collection

EUREKA

DELANEY & YOUNG
Face:	**DELANEY & YOUNG**
Reverse:	Blank
Bottom:	Blank
Color:	Aqua
Circa:	1903 – 1914
Location:	Eureka, Cal.
arity:	Extremely Rare
Value:	$ _____
Markota:	Unlisted

Proprietors Peter Delaney & Can Young bottled soda at 318 F Street then moving to 424 Third Street.

Facsimile of Delaney & Young bottle without Eureka or Eureka Cal. On the bottle. This bottle has been seen by many Humboldt County collectors but I was unable to track down owner.

Facsimile of known Bottle

EUREKA

C. F. RILEY SODA WORKS

Face:	C.F. RILEY
Reverse:	Blank
Bottom:	Blank
Bottom:	Blank
Color:	Cobalt
Circa:	1880's – 1910
Location:	Eureka, San Jose & San Bernadino
Rarity:	Scarce Number 1
Value:	Aqua $_____ Blue $_____
	Cobalt $_____ Teal $_____
Markota:	Page 111

Charles F. Riley started in Tombstone Arizona Territory in 1882. Tucson & Tombstone directories ad appeared "Pioneer Soda Works, C. F. Riley & Co" Proprietor, Manufacturer of Soda Water, Ginger Ale, Syrups, Seltzer Siphon Water, Gums, Apollinaris, & Cider.

Tombstone, Arizona. Orders Taken from All Parts of The Territory. Satisfaction Guaranteed.

According to Wikipedia

Cobalt glass, ground cobalt silicate, known in the industry as "Smalt", is a pigment in glass and production of bottles.

The cobalt color intensifies the appearance of bottles making them more desirable and more expensive.

John Louder Collection

Bob & Arlene Hansen Collection

EUREKA

	C. F. RILEY SODA WORKS
Face:	C.F. RILEY
Reverse:	Blank
Bottom:	Blank
Bottom:	Blank
Color:	Teal Green
Circa:	1880's – 1910
Location:	Eureka, San Jose & San Bernadino
Rarity:	Scarce Number 1
Value:	Aqua $_____ Blue $_____
	Cobalt $_____ Teal $_____
Markota:	Page 111

Charles F. Riley started in Tombstone Arizona Territory in 1882. Tucson & Tombstone directories ad appeared "Pioneer Soda Works, C. F. Riley & Co" Proprietor, Manufacturer of Soda Water, Ginger Ale, Syrups, Seltzer Siphon Water, Gums, Apollinaris, & Cider

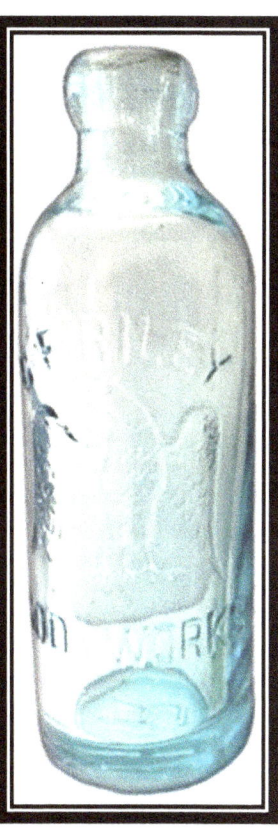

Left – Steve & Christie Curtiss Collection
Right - Bob & Arlene Hansen Collection

EUREKA

	C. F. RILEY SODA WORKS
Face:	C.F. RILEY & Co.
	Eagle
	SODA WORKS
Reverse:	Blank
Bottom:	Blank
Bottom:	R
Color:	Aqua
Circa:	1880's – 1910
Location:	Eureka, San Jose & San Bernadino
Rarity:	Scarce Number 2
Value:	Aqua $_____ Blue $_____
	Cobalt $_____ Teal $_____
Markota:	Page 111

In 1883-84 the directory stated his residence at Toughnut Street corner of Summer, proprietor of Pioneer Soda Works. In 1970 a cracked siphon bottle was dug with acid etched "C. F. RILEY, TOMBSTONE, A.T."

Steve & Christie Curtiss Collection

EUREKA

C. F. RILEY SODA WORKS

Face: C.F. RILEY
                    Eagle
                 SODA WORKS

Reverse: Blank
Bottom: R
Color: Aqua
Circa: 1880's – 1910
Location: Eureka, San Jose & San Bernadino
Rarity: Rare Number 3
Value: Aqua $_____ Blue $_____
               Cobalt $_____ Teal $_____
Markota: Page 111

Leaving Arizona he headed for Eureka, California in 1885 then to San Bernadino in 1887 and then San Jose in the 1890's.

An advertisement appeared in the Humboldt Daily Times January 1, 1885 reading "Eagle Soda Works, C. F. Riley & Co. Proprietors corner B & Cedar Streets, Eureka."
                 Notice shoulders.

Bob & Arlene Hansen Collection

EUREKA

C. F. RILEY SODA WORKS

Face: C.F. RILEY
           Different shaped Eagle
                 SODA WORKS

Reverse: Blank
Bottom: BOTTLE NEVER SOLD
                      R
               MUST BE RETURNED
Color: Teal Green
Circa: 1880's – 1910
Location: Eureka, San Jose & San Bernadino
Rarity: Rare Number 4
Value: Aqua $_____ Blue $_____
               Cobalt $_____ Teal $_____
Markota: Page 111

In the late 1880's & 1890's Riley was listed as proprietor of Eagle Soda Works San Bernadino and in the 1890's Charles & Louis Riley listed as Charles F. Riley & Co., Eagle Bottling Works, 613 South Pine Street, San Jose, California.

Bob & Arlene Hansen Collection

EUREKA

Testimonial for Humboldt Water.

To: J. P. Monroe, Manager
Good Roads Bottling Co.

Dear Sir. This is to certify that I have used Humboldt Water from the mineral spring of Flanagan, **Brosnan** & Co. in this city, and was cured of s deranged stomach by its use. I have drunk the water freely for about ten days and must say that its beneficial action upon the stomach and kidneys is wonderful. I have drunk from the mineral springs of the National Park in Montana and Wyoming, also Shasta and Apollinaris as now sold in this market, and in my humble judgment HUMBOLDT WATER beats them all. J. P. Murphy.   Eureka, Cal, Oct 11,1891

Flanigan & Brosnan owned and operated a mill in Humboldt. Timothy Brosnan committed suicide in 1908 by jumping off a ship.
     Humboldt Times October 1908

John Burton Collection

FERNDALE

  MONROE CIDER & VINEGAR FERNDALE

Face:	MONROE CIDER & VINEGAR CO. FERNDALE CAL.
Reverse:	Blank
Bottom:	Blank
Color:	Aqua
Circa:	1895 - 1905
Location:	Ferndale, Cal.
Rarity:	Rare
Value:	$ _____
Markota:	Page 84

Son Charles A. Monroe was in charge of the Monroe Cider & Vinegar plant in Ferndale located at North Main Street.

FORTUNA

  MONROE BOTTLING WORKS FORTUNA

Face:	MONROE BOTTLING WORKS FORTUNA, CAL.
Reverse:	Blank
Bottom:	Blank
Color:	Aqua
Circa:	1898 - 1899
Location:	Fortuna, Ca.
Rarity:	Scarce
Value:	$ _____
Markota:	Page 83

Son Charles A. Monroe also was in charge of the Monroe Bottling Works in Fortuna as well as the Ferndale operation.

Steve & Christie Curtiss Collection

Left – Steve & Christie Curtiss Collection
Right – Bob & Allene Hansen Collection

FORT BRAGG

STANDARD BOTTLING COMPANY

Face:	**STANDARD BOTTLING CO. FORT BRAGG**
Reverse:	Blank
Bottom:	P.C.G.W. and/or CCC
Color:	Aqua
Circa:	1905 – 1920
Location:	Fort Bragg, Cal.
Rarity:	Semi Common
Value:	$_____
Markota:	Page 130

C. H. Plummer started the Standard Bottling Works in 1905 selling the business to W. F. Kemppe in 1915. Kemppe bottled until the early 1920's.

John Burton Collection

Steve & Christie Curtiss purchased the blue STANDARD/ BOTTLING CO. / FORT BRAGG Over 30 years ago.

Steve & Christie Curtiss Collection

FRESNO

RICHTER'S BOTTLING WORKS

Face:	RICHTER'S BOTTLING WORKS FRESNO, CAL.
Reverse:	Blank
Bottom:	Some have R or a Diamond
Color:	Aqua and Clear
Circa:	1895 – 1920
Location:	Fresno, Cal.
Rarity:	Scarce
Value:	$_____
Markota:	Page 110

Jacob Richter started Richter's Bottling Works in 1895 at 701 I Street. He became the agent for Buffalo Brewery, Rainier Beer, Jacksons Napa Soda Water as well as a wholesale dealer in cigars, wines and liquors. He also had a line of temperance drinks.

Steve & Christie Curtiss Collection

RESNO

RICHTER'S BOTTLING WORKS

Face:	RICHTER'S BOTTLING WORKS FRESNO CALA.
Reverse:	Blank
Bottom:	Some have R or X or a Diamond
Color:	Aqua & Light Green
Circa:	1895 – 1920
Location:	Fresno, Cal.
Rarity:	Scarce
Value:	$_____ Clear & Aqua
Value:	$_____ Light Green
Markota:	Page 110

John Burton Collection

FRESNO

MORIMOTO SODA WORKS

Face: **MORIMOTO SODA WORKS**
Japanese Characters
FRESNO, CAL.

Reverse: Blank
Bottom: **P. C. G. W.** or **M**
Color: Aqua, Clear & Sun color
Circa: 1906 – 1925
Locality: Fresno, Cal.
Rarity: Scarce
Value: $_____
Markota: Page 85

Tsurikichi Morimoto started the soda works in 1906 at 844 F Street. In 1910 he moved to 827 F Street listed as a bottler of various flavors.

In 1926 a distant relative Hisajiro Kimura became a partner and the business name became Morimoto & Kimura Bottling Works. Morimoto sold in 1929 and Kimura changed the name to Rose Bottling Works.

Steve & Christie Curtiss Collection

Steve & Christie Curtiss Collection

FRESNO

CALIFORNIA SODA WORKS

Face:	CALIFORNIA SODA WORKS
	FRESNO, CAL.
Reverse:	Clank
Bottom:	Blank
Color:	Aqua
Circa:	1912 - 1916
Location:	Fresno, Cal.
Rarity:	Extremely Rare
Value:	$_____
Markota:	Page 24

Tahara & K. Yamamoto established both the California Soda Works at 1044 H Street and the San Joaquin Soda Water Works at 921 F Street with both having the same phone number; China 151. In 1914 T. Okada joined the partnership as a partner until 1916.

Steve & Christie Curtiss Collection

FRESNO

SAN JOAQUIN SODA WATER WORKS

Face:	SAN JOAQUIN SODA WATER WORKS
	SJSW
	FRESNO
	CAL.
Reverse:	Blank
Bottom:	Blank
Color:	Aqua
Circa:	1912 – 1916
Locality:	Fresno
Rarity:	Extremely Rare
Value:	$_____
Markota:	Page 118

In 1916 with both bottling plants closed down, K. Yamamoto partnered S. Kojima at 1435 Tulare Street in the dry goods business. Both Tahara & Okada apparently left Fresno. All addresses were in an area known as Chinatown.

Steve & Christie Curtiss Collection

FULLERTON

G. B. HUGGANS BOTTLING WORKS

Face:	G. B. HUGGANS FULLERTON CAL.
Reverse:	Blank
Bottom:	Some have an X
Color:	Aqua
Circa:	1899 – 1905
Locality:	Fullerton, Cal.
Rarity:	Rare
Value:	$_____
Markota:	Page 63

G. B. Huggans was proprietor of the Hotel Reception and the Temperance Bottling Works. He manufactured various flavors of soda however it is believed that he quit the soda business in 1903.

Steve & Christie Curtiss Collection

GILROY

GILROY SODA WORKS

Face:	T. HILDEBRAND GILROY CAL.
Reverse:	Blank
Bottom:	H
Color:	Aqua
Circa:	1884 -1888
Locality:	Gilroy, Cal.
Rarity:	Rare
Value:	$_____
Markota:	Page 62

Thomas H. Hildebrand started the Gilroy Soda Works in 1884 at Second Street north of Fitzgerald's Stable. He bottled various flavor soda water, sarsaparilla and cider until 1888 when he sold out to Daniel Williams.

Steve & Christie Curtiss Collection

GRASS VALLEY
W.E. DEAMER NEVADA SODA WATER CO.

Face:	W.E. DEAMER
Reverse:	GRASS VALLEY CAL.
Variant:	Also comes in blob top
Bottom:	GRAVITATING STOPPER MADE BY JOHN MATTHEWS PAT. OCT. 11, 1864 NEW YORK
Color:	Aqua
Circa:	1870 - 1890
Locality:	Grass Valley, Cal.
Rarity:	Common
Value:	$_____
Markota:	Page 34

W. E. Deamer's Nevada Soda Water Company was located at the corner of School & Richardson Streets manufacturing ginger ale, soda water and cider. Prior to 1880 it is believed that is when he used blob top bottles.

John Burton Collection

GRASS VALLEY
W.E. DEAMER NEVADA SODA WATER CO.

Face:	W.E. DEAMER
Reverse:	NEVADA SODA WATER Co. GRASS VALLEY NEVADA Co. CAL.
Variant:	Also comes in blob top
Bottom:	GRAVITATING STOPPER MADE BY JOHN MATTHEWS PAT. OCT. 11, 1864 NEW YORK
Color:	Aqua and Light Green
Circa:	1870 - 1890
Locality:	Grass Valley, Cal.
Rarity:	Common
Value:	$_____
Markota:	Page 35

Steve & Christie Curtiss Collection

GRASS VALLEY
R. H. WILLIAMS SODA WORKS

Face:	R.H. WILLIAMS
	GRASS VALLEY
Reverse:	Blank
Bottom:	330 H
Color:	Aqua
Circa:	1893 – 1915
Locality:	Grass Valley, Cal.
Rarity:	Semi Rare
Value:	$_____
Markota:	Page 144

In 1893 Richard H. Williams purchased the Alta Soda Works located on the corner of Auburn & Race Streets from Shaw & Bennett. Son William Williams joined his father manufacturing temperance drinks until 1915. Richard continued in the grocery business and William went to work for Sperry Flour Company of Nevada County.

Steve & Christie Curtiss Collection

GRASS VALLEY
HANSSEN BROS. SODA WORKS

Face:	HANSSEN BROS.
	G. W. B.
	GRASS VALLEY, CAL.
Reverse:	Blank
Bottom:	+
Color:	Aqua
Circa:	1894 – 1900
Locality:	Grass Valley, Cal.
Rarity:	Scarce
Value:	$_____
Markota:	Page 58

Henry H. Hanssen founded the Golden West Bottlery which was the former Grass Valley Soda Works about 1894. Brother Harry joined the firm in 1896 continuing to manufacture soda water, sarsaparilla, siphon water and beer.

The company was also known as GRASS VALLEY SODA WORKS. Henry died in 1898 and his wife Catherine managed with Harry until 1900 when Harry became the sole owner continuing for a few more years.

Steve & Christie Curtiss Collection

GRIDLEY

	GRIDLEY SODA WORKS
Face:	GRIDLEY
	CAL.
	SODA WORKS
Reverse:	Blank
Bottom:	G. N. D.
Color:	Aqua
Circa:	1888 – 1901
Location:	Gridley, Cal.
Rarity:	Extremely Rare
Value:	$_____
Markota:	Page 52

Asa Keene founded the Gridley Soda Works in 1888 and the building was located at the corner of Hazel & Vermont.

Steve & Christie Curtiss Collection

GRIDLEY

	GRIDLEY SODA WORKS
Face:	GRIDLEY
	SODA WORKS
Reverse:	Blank
Bottom:	G. N. D.
Color:	Aqua
Circa:	1888 – 1901
Location:	Gridley, Cal.
Rarity:	Rare
Value:	$_____
Markota:	Page 52

Steve & Christie Curtiss Collection

HALF MOON BAY
        HALF MOON BAY SODA WATER CO.

Face: HALF MOON BAY
                   SODA WATER CO.
                   HALF MOON BAY
                        CAL.

Reverse: Blank
Bottom: Blank
Color: Aqua
Circa: 1905 – 1910
Locality: Miramar, Half Moon Bay, Cal.
Rarity: Extremely Rare
Value: $_____
Markota: Page 56

Located in the town of Miramar, Lorne F. Roe, proprietor manufactures sweet soda and syphon soda also offers Napa Water, Bartlett Mineral Water and various syrups.

Not sure of this bottle in Markota's book.
I believe that this is an image of a crown top

Believed to be a crown top

HANFORD
        J. W. CAMP

Face: J. W. CAMP
Reverse: Blank
Bottom: Blank
Color: Aqua
Circa: Late 1890's
Locality: Hanford, Kings County
Rarity: Extremely Rare
Value: $_____
Markota: Unlisted

Researched J. W. Camp without success regarding soda water. Paper mentioned that he became a Justice of the Peace after he retired from business about 1901.

Image from Hutch Book.Com

HANFORD

HANFORD SODA WORKS

Face:	HANFORD SODA WORKS J. S.
Reverse:	Blank
Bottom:	Blank
Color:	Aqua
Circa:	1895 - 1902
Location:	Hanford, Cal.
Rarity:	Scarce
Value:	$_____
Markota:	Page 57

Joseph Schnereger founded the Hanford Soda Works in 1895 located at 119 South Douty Street.

The business was moved to 305 East Sixth Street and Thomas Downing became a partner well into the 1920's.

HANFORD

HANFORD ICE COMPANY

Face:	HANFORD ICE CO. HANFORD CAL.
Reverse:	Blank
Bottom:	Blank
Color:	Aqua
Circa:	1895 - 1902
Location:	Hanford, Cal.
Rarity:	Rare
Value:	$_____
Markota:	Page 57

John Burton Collection

Steve & Christie Curtiss Collection

HAYWARD

	HAYWARDS SODA WORKS
Face:	HAYWARDS
	J. A. COLLINS
	SODA WORKS
Reverse:	Blank
Bottom:	C
Color:	Aqua
Circa:	1886 - 1890
Locality:	Hayward, Cal
Rarity:	Rare
Value:	$_____
Markota:	Page 58

James A. Collins operated the soda works until 1886 when Simon J. Simons joined in partnership. Collins returned to his former employment with Central Pacific Railroad & Western Union Telegraph.

Steve & Christie Curtiss Collection

HAYWARD

	HAYWARDS SODA WORKS
Face:	HAYWARDS
	S. J. SIMMONS
	SODA WORKS
Reverse:	Blank
Bottom:	Blank
Color:	Aqua
Circa:	1890 - 1920
Locality:	Hayward, Cal
Rarity:	Scarce
Value:	$_____
Markota:	Page 589

Simmons became sole owner of the soda works after purchasing it from James Collins who returned to his former employment with the railroad & telegraph companies.

John Burton Collection

HEALDSBURG

          F.O. BRANDT HEALDSBURG
Face: F. B.
                 HEALDSBURG
                 CAL.

Reverse;   Blank
Bottom: Some blank or have 328 H
Color: Aqua
Circa: 1885 – 1918
Locality: Healdsburg, Cal.
Rarity: Semi Common
Value: $_____
Markota: Page 48

Frederick Otto Brandt started the bottling works on University Street between Matheson & North Streets. Brandt also bottled beer from Buffalo, Enterprise and National breweries. He never was a brewer.

John Burton Collection

HEALDSBURG

          F.O. BRANDT HEALDSBURG
Face: F. B.
                 HEALDSBURG

Reverse;   Blank
Bottom: Some blank or have B or 328 H
Color: Aqua
Circa: 1885 – 1918
Locality: Healdsburg, Cal.
Rarity: Semi Common
Value: $_____
Markota: Page 48

Brandt's local competition was from Carl Mueller who was located on the corner of North & West Streets. Mueller had a beer garden and sold his beer to local saloons in kegs. Mueller never bottled soda.

John Burton Collection

HOLLISTER

HOLLISTER SODA WORKS
Face: J. DORN
               SODA WORKS
Reverse: Blank
Bottom: Blank
Color: Aqua
Circa: 1883 – 1890
Location: Hollister, Cal.
Rarity: Rare
Value: $_____
Markota: Unlisted

Dorn was listed as proprietor of the Hollister Soda Works manufacturing soda water, sarsaparilla, ginger ale, iron and cider.

Steve & Christie Curtiss Collection

HOLLISTER

HOLLISTER SODA WORKS
Face: HOLLISTER
               J. DORN
               SODA WORKS
Reverse: Blank
Bottom: Blank
Color: Aqua
Circa: 1883 – 1890
Location: Hollister, Cal.
Rarity: Rare
Value: $_____
Markota: Page 63

Steve & Christie Curtiss Collection

JACKSON

           JACKSON BOTTLING WORKS
Face: JACKSON BOTTLING
               P & G monogram
               WORKS
Reverse: Blank
Bottom: Blank
Color: Aqua
Circa: 1900 – 1909
Locality: Jackson, Cal.
Rarity: Scarce
Value: $_____
Markota: Page 67

Unable to verify this was a hutch bottle and believe that it may have been a crown top rubbing in Markota's book as someone may have told him they had heard rumor there was a hutch.

Podesta & Tallon started in 1900 when crown tops were replacing hutch bottles and it would make sense that they would install crown top bottling machinery.

Frank Podesta & Henry Tallon started Jackson Bottling Works on North Main Street. Podesta had heart problems and left the firm in 1909.

It is believed that the "G" in the monogram was a misprint and should have been a "T".

JAMESTOWN

           SAMMONS BROS. JAMESTOWN
Face: SAMMONS BROS
               JAMESTOWN
Reverse;   Blank
Bottom: X
Color: Aqua
Circa: 1894 – 1900
Locality: Jamestown, Cal. Tuolumne Co.
Rarity: Scarce
Value: $_____
Markota: Page 114

Brothers John & Henry Sammons started the Sammons Brothers Soda Works around 1894 and in 1900 Henry left and started his soda water business in Sonora. Henry sold the Sonora Bottling Works to John Bacon in 1908.

Steve & Christie Curtiss Collection

KESWICK

FINK & MUGLER BOTTLING WORKS

Face:	**FINK & MUGLER**
	BOTTLERS
	KESWICK, CAL.
Reverse:	Blank
Bottom:	Blank
Color:	Aqua
Circa:	1901 – 1909
Locality:	Keswick, Cal. Shasta County
Rarity:	Extremely Rare
Value:	$_____
Markota:	Page 49

William Fink & Peter Mugler owned the Keswick Bottling works and sold to Henry Watson in 1909. Peter Mugler also bottled Beer.

Steve & Christie Curtiss Collection

KING CITY

KING CITY SODA WORKS

Face:	**P. E. WEAVER**
	KING CITY
	SODA WORKS
Reverse:	Blank
Bottom:	Blank
Color:	Aqua
Circa:	1898 - 1905
Locality:	King City, Cal. Monterey, Co.
Rarity:	Extremely Rare
Value:	$_____
Markota:	Page 141

Established by P. E. Weaver in King City, Monterey County, in 1898. He manufactured various flavors of soda water until 1905.

Steve & Christie Curtiss Collection

LIVERMORE

LIVERMORE SODA WORKS

Face:	LIVERMORE SODA WORKS
Reverse:	Blank
Bottom:	33
Color:	Aqua
Circa:	1876 – 1985
Locality:	Livermore, Cal. Alameda Co.
Rarity:	Rare
Value:	$_____
Markota:	Page 71

A man last name Wallis started the Livermore soda works on L Street between First & Second Streets. Through the years the location changed numerous times. In 1880 the Gordimer brothers are listed as operation the soda works at Oak & Livermore Avenue.

In 1887 the listing is the corner of Chestnut & Livermore with E. & J. Berg as owners. In 1889 they sold to Julius Jacob moving to K Street between 6th & 7th Streets. 1902 Warren Lamb purchased the business. The building was consumed by fire in 1985.

**Steve & Christie Curtiss Collection
Including photo**

LIVERMORE

	LIVERMORE SODA WORKS
Face:	LIVERMORE SODA WORKS
	LIVERMORE
	CALA.
Reverse:	Blank
Bottom:	7 or large dot
Color:	Aqua
Circa:	1890's
Locality:	Livermore, Cal. Alameda, Co.
Rarity:	Scarce
Value:	$_____
Markota:	Page 72

**Steve & Christie Curtiss Collection
Including photo**

LIVERMORE

LIVERMORE SODA WORKS

Face: LIVERMORE SODA WORKS
LIVERMORE
CAL.
Reverse: Blank
Bottom: 7 or large dot
Color: Aqua
Circa: 1900
Locality: Livermore, Cal. Alameda, Co.
Rarity: Rare
Value: $_____
Markota: Page 72

**Steve & Christie Curtiss Collection
Including photo**

Livermore Soda Works Circa 1910

LIVERMORE

LIVERMORE SODA WORKS

Face:	LIVERMORE SODA WORKS
	Lamb monogram
	LIVERMORE
	CAL.
Reverse:	Blank
Bottom:	Blank
Color:	Aqua
Circa:	1902 - 1910
Locality:	Livermore, Cal. Alameda, Co.
Rarity:	Extremely Rare
Value:	$_____
Markota:	Page 72

Warren Lamb was proprietor at this time from 1902 – 1910.

Steve & Christie Curtiss Collection

LODI

LODI SODA WORKS

Face:	LODI
	SODA WORKS
Reverse:	Blank
Bottom:	Blank
Color:	Aqua
Circa:	1880 - 1918
Locality:	Lodi, Cal. San Joaquin Co.
Rarity:	Common
Value:	$_____
Markota	Page 73

Andrew J. Larsen started the Lodi Soda Works & Ice Depot in the early 1880's on Sacramento Street corner of Walnut. He also owned a livery stable but was the local undertaker. In 1887 James Cook became a partner in the soda works until 1900.

In 1900 Charles Stollars & Edward Hevey were the new proprietors until 1904 when Hevey left and Charles expanded selling coal, ice and soda waters. Charles died in 1911 and his widow Anna operated the business until 1918.

Steve & Christie Curtiss Collection

LOS ANGELES

        LOS ANGELES
            (Star)
        SODA WORKS
        (Rolled "R")
        Whittled 2-piece mold

Reverse:	Blank
Bottom:	
Color:	Aqua
Circa:	1884
Locality:	Los Angeles, Cal.
Rarity:	Extremely Rare
Value:	$_____
Markota:	Page 74 Bottle number 2

In 1890 the Stoll's moved to 509 Commercial Street still bottling soda water, sarsaparilla, and ginger ale until 1898 when Phillip died.

Steve & Christie Curtiss Collection

LOS ANGELES

        LOS ANGELES SODA WORKS

Face:	LOS ANGELES
	(Star)
	SODA WORKS
	THIS BOTTLE
	IS REGISTERED
	NOT TO BE SOLD
	Two-piece mold
Reverse:	Blank
Bottom:	STAR
Base:	Blank
Color:	Clear & Aqua
Circa:	1867 – 1924
Locality:	Los Angeles, Cal.
Rarity:	Rare
Value:	$_____
Markota:	Page 74 Bottle number 1

Los Angeles Soda Works was established in 1872 by W. H. Stoll & W. H. Huber at 13 Aliso Street. Huber stayed until 1875 and Stoll became the sole owner.

In 1884 Stoll moved the business to 107 Sansevain Street Also in 1884 Henry Stoll took on Phillip C. Stoll, probably his brother, as a partner.

Eddie Kuskie Collection

LOS ANGELES

                LOS ANGELES
                   (Star)
                SODA WORKS
                (Rolled "R")
       Squatty slug plate 2-piece mold

Reverse:	Blank
Bottom:	Star
Color:	Aqua
Circa:	1890
Locality:	Los Angeles, Cal.
Rarity:	Extremely Rare
Value:	$_____
Markota:	Page 74 Bottle number 3

Henry Stoll continued as proprietor until he died in 1906. Henry's family continued the business until 1925 when they sold to F. P. & F. R. Bray who also bottled "Brays Special Extra Dry" beer.

Henry W. Stoll also was the owner of the Pasadena Soda Works located at 762 South Fair Oaks Boulevard from 1884 until 1919.

LOS ANGELES

                LOS ANGELES
                   (Star)
                SODA WORKS
       Slug plate 2-piece mold

Reverse:	Blank
Bottom:	Star
Color:	Aqua
Circa:	1890
Locality:	Los Angeles, Cal.
Rarity:	Extremely Rare
Value:	$_____
Markota:	Page 75 Bottle number 4

Steve & Christie Curtiss Collection

Steve & Christie Curtiss Collection

LOS ANGELES

LOS ANGELES
Trade (Star) Mark
SODA WORKS
Whittled applied top 2-piece mold

Reverse:	Blank
Bottom:	Star
Color:	Aqua
Circa:	1890
Locality:	Los Angeles, Cal.
Rarity:	Extremely Rare
Value:	$_____
Markota:	Page 75 Bottle number 5

The **Los Angeles Soda Works** H. W. Stoll & Company, proprietors, 509 Commercial Street, uses only the celebrated Poland Rock Natural Mineral Water for the manufacture of all carbonated drinks. Call for their Soda, Selzer, Ginger Ale and. Sarsaparilla and Iron. All goods are of the finest quality, and for purity and flavor cannot be excelled.
Los Angeles Herald – September 5, 1890

John Burton Collection

LOS ANGELES

LOS ANGELES
Trade (Star) Mark
SODA WORKS
THIS BOTTLE
IS REGISTERED
NOT TO BE SOLD

Reverse:	Blank
Bottom:	Star
Color:	Aqua
Circa:	1890 - 1924
Locality:	Los Angeles, Cal.
Rarity:	Extremely Rare
Value:	$_____
Markota:	Page 75 Bottle number 6

H. W. Stoll & Company were also agents for Maier & Zobelein, Los Angeles Brewing Company, Rainier Brewing Company and Mathie Brewing Company.
Los Angeles Herald – June 1906

John Burton Collection

LOS ANGELES

CALIFORNIA SODA WORKS

Face:	CALIFORNIA
	S.C.& Co.
	SODA WORKS
Reverse:	Blank
Bottom:	WIS. G. Co. / Milw.
Color:	Aqua & Lime Green
Circa:	1884 1884
Locality:	Los Angeles, Cal.
Rarity:	Aqua Rare
Value:	$_____
	Lime Green Extremely Rare
Value:	$_____
Markota:	Page 22

Save Celestine started the California soda Works at 250 Aliso Street. He had been in the livery stable business.

WIS. G. Co. / Milw.
Wisconsin Glass Co. Milwaukee Wisconsin

Eddie Kuskie Collection

LOS ANGELES

CALIFORNIA SODA WORKS

Face:	CALIFORNIA
	S.C.& Co.
	SODA WORKS
Reverse:	Blank
Bottom:	WIS. G. Co. / Milw.
Color:	Aqua & Lime Green
Circa:	1884 1884
Locality:	Los Angeles, Cal.
Rarity:	Aqua Rare
Value:	$_____
	Lime Green Extremely Rare
Value:	$_____
Markota:	Page 22

Save Celestine started the California soda Works at 250 Aliso Street. He had been in the livery stable business.

WIS. G. Co. / Milw.
Wisconsin Glass Co. Milwaukee Wisconsin

Eddie Kuskie Collection

LOS ANGELES

CALIFORNIA SODA WORKS

Face:	CALIFORNIA
	S.C.& Co.
	SODA WORKS
Reverse:	Blank
Bottom:	WIS. G. Co. / Milw.
Color:	Aqua & Lime Green
Circa:	1884 1884
Locality:	Los Angeles, Cal.
Rarity:	Aqua Rare
Value:	$_____
	Lime Green Extremely Rare
Value:	$_____
Markota:	Page 22

Left - John Burton Collection
Right - Steve & Christie Curtiss Collection

LOS ANGELES

PACIFIC SODA WORKS

Face:	PACIFIC
	(Anchor)
	SODA WORKS
	L. A. CAL.
	Taller bottle 2-piece Hutch
Base:	10-Sided panel
Reverse:	THIS BOTTLE IS NEVER SOLD
Bottom:	Blank
Color:	Aqua
Circa:	1888 - 1893
Locality:	Los Angeles, Cal.
Rarity:	Extremely Rare
Value:	$_____
Markota:	Page 97

William Lammerson, Christ Kiesner & Bernard Spilker started the Pacific Soda Works at 714 Temple Street. Christ left the company in 1891 and the other two continued until 1893.

Lammerson went to work as a bricklayer and Spilker went to work as a bottler for Pacific Bottling Works for Frederick Hoppe.

Steve & Christie Curtiss Collection

LOS ANGELES

PACIFIC SODA WORKS

Face: PACIFIC
        Anchor (Tilted left)
        SODA WORK
        L. A. CAL.
        2-Piece mold rare variant
Base: 10-Sided panel
Reverse: THIS BOTTLE IS NEVER SOLD
Bottom: Blank
Color: Aqua
Circa: 1888 - 1893
Locality: Los Angeles, Cal.
Rarity: Rare
Value: $_____
Markota: Page 97 - 98

Steve & Christie Curtiss Collection

LOS ANGELES

PACIFIC SODA WORKS

Face: PACIFIC
        Anchor (Tilted right)
        SODA WORKS
        L. A. CAL.
        2 – Piece crude whittled
        Slug plate & applied top mold
Base: 10-Sided panel
Reverse: THIS BOTTLE IS NEVER SOLD
Bottom: Blank
Color: Aqua
Circa: 1888 - 1893
Locality: Los Angeles, Cal.
Rarity: Extremely Rare
Value: $_____
Markota: Page 97- 98

Steve & Christie Curtiss Collection

LOS ANGELES
PACIFIC BOTTLING WORKS

Face:	**PACIFIC**
	Anchor (Tilting left)
	L.A. CAL.
	BOTTLING WORKS
Base:	10 – Sided panel
Reverse:	Blank
Bottom:	Blank
Color:	Pale Aqua
Circa:	1891 – 1898
Locality:	Los Angeles, Cal.
Rarity:	Extremely Rare
Value:	$_____
Markota:	97 - 98

Frederick Hoppe proprietor of a saloon, lodging house & the Pacific Bottling Works. The bottling works in competition with Pacific Soda Works was located at the northeast corner of 3rd & Los Angeles Street.

He also bottled beer for Maier & Zobelein, bottled mineral water and dealt in fountains. In 1885 he moved to 446-466 Wolfskill Street being a wholesale dealer in wines and liquors. In 1887 he's listed as the proprietor of the Schlitz Saloon on Spring Street closing businesses in 1898.

Eddie Kuskie Collection

LOS ANGELES
EXCELSIOR SODA WORKS

Face:	**EXCELSIOR**
	SODA WORKS
	LOS
	ANGELES, CAL.
	(Slug plate with large embossing)
Reverse:	Blank
Bottom:	**C. B. S.**
Color:	Aqua
Circa:	1886 -1920
Locality:	Los Angeles, Cal.
Rarity:	Rare
Value:	$_____
Markota:	Page 47

Steve & Christie Curtiss Collection

LOS ANGELES
EXCELSIOR SODA WORKS

Face:	EXCELSIOR SODA WORKS LOS ANGELES, CAL. With & without slug plate Taller of the two bottles & smaller embossing
Reverse:	Blank
Bottom:	T. S.
Color:	Aqua
Circa:	1886 -1920
Locality:	Los Angeles, Cal.
Rarity:	Rare
Value:	$_____
Markota:	Page 47

Founded by Thomas Strohm & E. H. May in 1896 corner of 2nd & Vine Streets. May left soon in 1886 & Strohm operated alone until 1905. Relocating to 323 Town Avenue he retired in 1905 and Clarence Strohm became the new owner again moving a few times landing at 1331 Willow Street.

Steve & Christie Curtiss Collection

LOS ANGELES
JAMES SODA WORKS

Face:	JAMES SODA WORKS LOS ANGELES CAL.
Reverse:	Blank
Bottom:	X
Color:	Aqua
Circa:	1892 - 1898
Location:	Los Angeles, Cal.
Rarity:	Rare
Value:	$_____
Markota:	Page 68

Apparently, William J. James started bottling in his garage. He was an analytical & consulting chemist bottling ginger ale in Codd type bottles.
Codd bottles are embossed with:

Steve & Christie Curtiss Collection

LOS ANGELES

JAMES SODA WORKS

Face: **JAMES**
SODA WORKS
LOS ANGELES, CAL.

Reverse: Blank
Bottom: Blank
Color: Aqua
Circa: 1892 - 1898
Location: Los Angeles, Cal.
Rarity: Extremely Rare
Value: $_____
Markota: Page 68

In 1892 James sold to Edward Dunbar & Frederick Winstanley still located at the original location, corner 11th & Overton Streets. They closed the soda works in 1898

Steve & Christie Curtiss Collection

LOS ANGELES

F. A. HEIM BOTTLING WORKS

Face: **F. A. HEIM**
LOS ANGELES CAL.
BOTTLING WORKS

Reverse: Blank
Bottom: **H. B. W.**
Color: Blue Aqua
Circa: 1898 – 1906
Location: Los Angeles, Cal.
Rarity: Semi Rare
Value: $_____
Markota: Page 59

Ferdinand A. Heim started at 446 Central Avenue moving to 401 Ramirez Street in 1889.

Steve & Christie Curtiss Collection

LOS ANGELES
F. A. HEIM BOTTLING WORKS

Face:	F. A. HEIM'S BOTTLING WORKS
Reverse:	Blank
Bottom:	H. B. S.
Color:	Blue Aqua
Circa:	1898 – 1906
Location:	Los Angeles, Cal.
Rarity:	Semi Rare
Value:	$_____
Markota:	Page 59

Steve & Christie Curtiss Collection

LOS ANGELES
F. A. HEIM BOTTLING WORKS

Face:	Embossed bottom only
Reverse:	Blank
Bottom:	HEIM'S
Color:	Blue Aqua
Circa:	1898 – 1906
Location:	Los Angeles, Cal.
Rarity:	Extremely Rare
Value:	$_____
Markota:	Page 60

LOS ANGELES
RAMONA BOTTLING WORKS

Face:	RAMONA BOTTLING WORKS LOS ANGELES, CAL.
Reverse:	Blank
Bottom:	P. S.
Color:	Aqua &Light lime Green
Circa:	1905 - 1909
Locality:	Los Angeles, Cal.
Rarity:	Scarce
Value:	$_____ Aqua
	$_____ Lime green
Markota:	Page 109

Ramona soda was bottled at 401 Ramírez Avenue at F. A. Hein's bottling plant was located. Hein was also the distributor of Ramona Mineral Water.

Paul Gessner founded the company however Gessner sold to Peter Sarrall in 1907.

Steve & Christie Curtiss Collection

LOS ANGELES
PURITAS DISTILLED WATER

Face:	Blank
Reverse:	Blank
Bottom:	PURITAS LOS ANGELES
Color:	Aqua
Circa:	1900 – 1910
Location:	Los Angeles, Cal.
Rarity:	Common
Value:	$_____
Markota:	Page 108

Puritas Distilled Water, Ice & Cold Storage company was located on East 7th & the Santa Fe Railroad tracks.

Los Angeles Ice & Cold Storage bought out Puritas Distilled Water Company in 1910 staying at the same location.

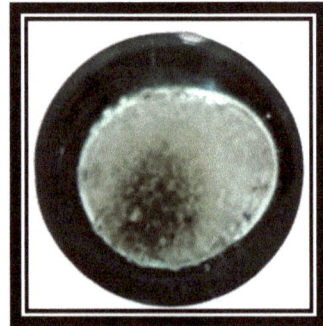

Steve & Christie Curtiss Collection

LOS ANGELES
SANITAS BOTTLING WORKS
Face:	SANITAS BOTTLING WORKS LOS ANGELES
Reverse:	Blank
Bottom:	Blank
Color:	Aqua
Circa:	1900 – 1905
Locality:	Los Angeles, Cal.
Rarity:	Rare
Value:	$_____
Markota:	119

No information regarding this bottling company. The closest I came to Sanitas Water was a Turkish bath in Sanitas.

Left – Steve & Christie Curtiss Collection
Right -Eddie Kuskie Collection

LOS ANGELES
LICHTER'S BOTTLING WORKS
Face:	LIGHTER'S BOTTLING WORKS LOS ANGELES, CAL.
Reverse:	Blank
Bottom:	Blank
Color:	Aqua
Circa:	1902 - 1905
Locality:	Los Angeles, Cal.
Rarity:	Extremely Rare
Value:	$_____
Markota:	Page 71

Lazarus Lichter started the bottling works in 1902 at 116½ San Pedro Street. In 1904 he moved to 1926 Daien Place closing in 1905

Left – Steve & Christie Curtiss Collection
Right -Eddie Kuskie Collection

LOS ANGELES

	CASCADE BOT. WKS.
Face:	CASCADE BOT. WKS.
	PEVERLY
	BROS. PROPS.
	LOS ANGLES
	Angeles misspelt
Reverse:	Blank
Bottom:	Blank
Base:	10-Sided panel
Color:	Aqua
Circa:	1907 – 1909
Locality:	Los Angeles, Cal.
Rarity:	Extremely Rare
Value:	$_____
Markota:	Page 25

Charles & George Peverly started Cascade Bottling Works at 2111 Vallejo Street closing in 1909.

A few years later they were listed as proprietors of Oxnard Soda Works manufacturing various flavored sodas and jobbers of chewing gum and distributors of Blue & Gold beer, as well as Anaheim bottled & draft beer.

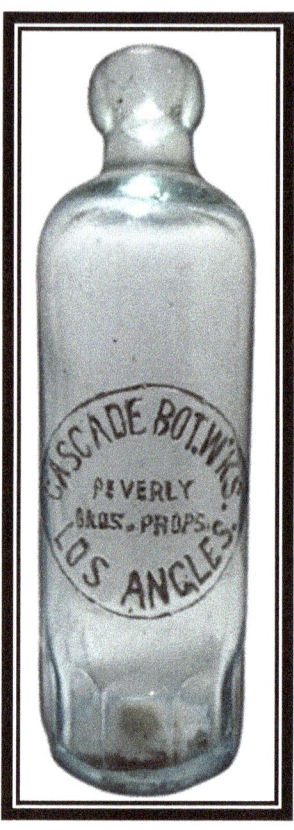

Steve & Christie Curtiss Collection

LOS ANGELES

	NEW YORK BOTTLING COMPANY
Face:	NEW YORK
	BOTTLING CO.
	J. SCHWARTZ, PROP.
	LOS ANGELES, CAL.
	This bottle is slug plate variant
	4-Piece mold
Reverse:	Blank
Bottom:	Blank
Color:	Aqua
Circa:	1906 – 1918
Locality:	Los Angeles, Cal.
Rarity:	Extremely Rare
Value:	$_____
Markota:	Page 91

Jacob Schwartz proprietor of the New York Bottling Works from 1906 t0 1918.

Steve & Christie Curtiss Collection

LOS ANGELES
NEW YORK BOTTLING COMPANY

Face:	NEW YORK BOTTLING WORKS LOS ANGELES CAL.

This bottle is a two-piece mold

Reverse:	7 – A.B. Co.
Bottom:	N. Y. B. W.
Front Base:	THIS BOTTLE NOT TO BE SOLD
Color:	Aqua
Circa:	1906 – 1918
Locality:	Los Angeles, Cal.
Rarity:	Extremely Rare
Value:	$_____
Markota:	Page 91

First located at 756 South San Pedro Street moving to 1235 East 8th Street then in 1917 to 1003 East Jefferson Boulevard.

In 1907 Schwartz had a partner, Max Russakov who only stayed one year.

Left – John Burton Collection
Right - Steve & Christie Curtiss Collection

LOS ANGELES
NEW YORK BOTTLING COMPANY

Face:	NEW YORK BOTTLING WORKS LOS ANGELES

This bottle is a two-piece mold

Reverse:	Blank
Bottom:	N. Y. B. W.
Color:	Aqua
Circa:	1906 – 1918
Locality:	Los Angeles, Cal.
Rarity:	Extremely Rare
Value:	$_____
Markota:	Page 91

Eddie Kuskie Collection

LOS ANGELES
CRYSTAL BOTTLING CO.

Face:	CRYSTAL BOTTLNG CO. LOS ANGELES, CA.
Reverse:	Blank
Bottom:	Monogram C B CO
Base:	THIS BOTTLE MUST NOT BE SOLD
Color:	Aqua
Circa:	1903 – 1910
Locality:	Los Angeles
Rarity:	Scarce
Value:	$_____
Markota:	Page 32

William Cooper & Elmer Miller started the Crystal Bottling Company at 627 North Main Street in 1903. In 1904 Cooper left the company and Charles Fife became a new partner. In 1905 Miller left and Herman Robsahm joined Fife moving to 402 Aliso Street closing 1810.

David Garcia Collection

LOS ANGELES
CRYSTAL BOTTLING CO. (Paper label)

Face:	CRYSTAL BOTTLNG CO. LOS ANGELES, CA.
Reverse:	Blank
Bottom:	Blank
Base:	Blank
Color:	Aqua
Circa:	1910 - 1918
Locality:	Los Angeles
Rarity:	Scarce
Value:	$_____
Markota:	Unlisted

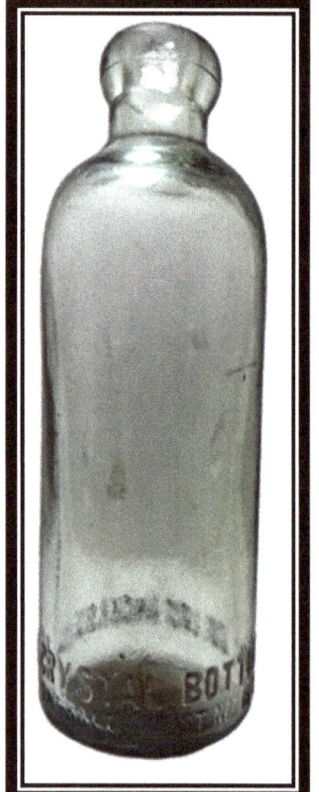 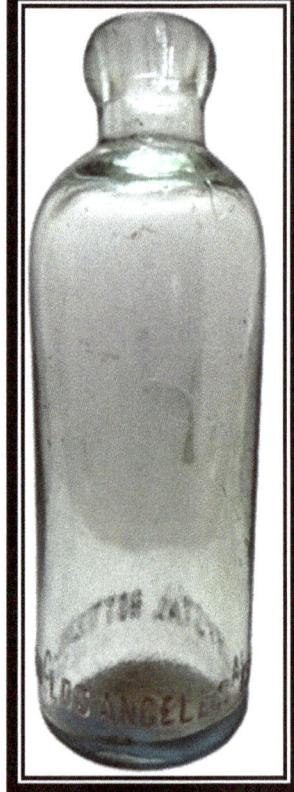

Steve & Christie Curtiss Collection

LOS ANGELES
HYGEIA MINERAL WATER COMPANY

Face:	HYGEIA MINERAL WATER CO. LOS ANGELES CAL.
Reverse:	Blank
Bottom:	HYGEIA
Color:	Aqua
Circa:	1907 – 1910
Locality:	Los Angeles
Rarity:	Rare
Value:	$_____
Markota:	Page 64

Fabian Barbanell started the Hygeia Mineral Water Company in 1907 at 958 East Pico Boulevard. As with his former San Francisco bottling works Los Angeles was short termed.

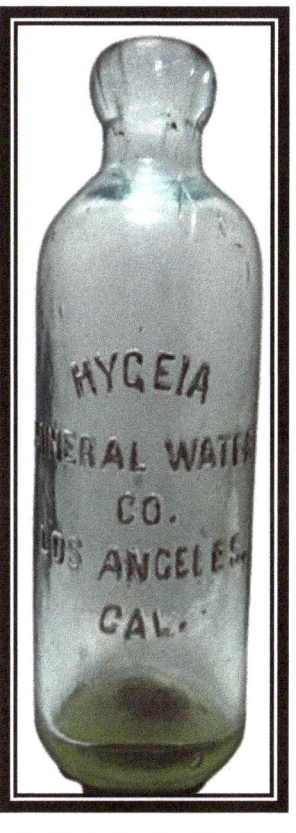

Steve & Christie Curtiss Collection

MADERA
BORELLO & PORTER SODA WORKS

Face:	BORELLO & PORTER MADERA
Reverse:	Blank
Bottom:	+
Color:	Aqua
Circa:	1890 – 1907
Locality:	Madera, Cal. Madera Co.
Rarity:	Rare
Value:	$_____
Markota:	Page 17

Frank Borello who was part owner of Fresno Soda Works & Grant J. Porter established the Madera Soda Works manufacturing various types of sodas and the bottled beer. Frank left the Madera Soda Works in 1907 and moved back to Fresno and Porter operated the business in Madera until mid-1920's.

Steve & Christie Curtiss Collection

MEDERA (Misspelt)
BORELLO & PORTER SODA WORKS

Face:	BORELLO & PORTER
	MEDERA
	Madera misspelt
Reverse:	Blank
Bottom:	+
Color:	Clear & Sun colored
Circa:	1890 – 1907
Locality:	Madera, Cal. Madera Co.
Rarity:	Extremely Rare
Value	$_____
Markota:	Page 17

Steve & Christie Curtiss Collection

MARYSVILLE
CHARLES BELDING SODA WORKS

Face:	CHAS. BELDING
	B
	MARYSVILLE
	SODA WORKS
Reverse:	Blank
Bottom:	Blank
Color:	Aqua
Circa:	1895 – 1910
Locality:	Marysville, Cal.
Rarity:	Extremely Rare
Value:	$_____

Steve & Christie Curtiss Collection

MARYSVILLE

        MARYSVILLE SODA WORKS

Face:	Blank
Reverse:	Blank
Bottom:	MARYSVILLE SODA WORKS
Color:	Aqua
Circa:	1905 – 1930
Locality:	Marysville, Cal.
Rarity:	Rare
Value:	$_____
Markota:	Page 77

A. G. Eames former owner of the Chico Soda Works & brother Henry acquired in 1905 the Marysville Soda Works established by Belden & Lippincott.

They manufactured various sodas & were agents for Jackson's Napa Soda, Cook's Spring Water, Richardson Spring Water, Bartlett Water, Castle Rock & Witter Springs Water. They also bottled beer for various breweries.

Steve & Christie Curtiss Collection

MARYSVILLE

Face:	B & Co. (Belden & Co.)
Reverse:	Blank
Bottom:	Blank:
Color:	Aqua
Circa:	1895 - 1910
Locality:	Marysville, Cal.
Rarity:	Rare
Value:	$_____
Markota:	Unlisted

Steve & Christie Curtiss Collection

MARYSVILLE & STOCKTON
B (Belding)
Face: B
Reverse: Blank
Bottom: GRAVITATING STOPPER MADE BY JOHN MATTHEWS PAT. OCT. 11, 1864 NEW YORK

Color: Aqua
Circa: 1870 – 1910
Locality: Marysville & Stockton
Rarity: Common
Value $_____
Markota: Page 9

Charles Belding worked for bottlers Lippincott & Vaughn in Stockton from 1852 to 1855. Belding partnered with another former employee of Lippincott & Vaughn purchasing the Murphy's Soda Works. Belden sold his interest a year later in 1856 returning to Stockton purchasing Vaughn's interest in Lippincott & Vaughn in 1857. The firm of Lippincott & Belding lasted until 1870 when Belding bought out Benjamin Lippincott.

Belding & Lippincott had also been partners in another soda works in Marysville from 1863 until 1894 when Belding became to sole owner. In 1895 this soda works was operated by Charles's brother Lyman.

At the same time in 1895 Belden sold part interest in the Stockton plant to Samuel B. Huskins with the company becoming known as Belden & Huskins Soda Works. Those bottles are embossed H & B M'VILLE. Charles Belding died February 17, 1905 and it appears all operations stopped in 1910.

With lines in letter B
Steve & Christie Curtiss Collection

No lines in letter B
Steve & Christie Curtiss Collection

MARYSVILLE

Face:	**H & B**
Reverse:	Blank
Bottom:	Blank
Color:	Aqua
Circa:	1895
Locality:	Marysville, Cal.
Rarity:	Rare
Value:	$_____
Markota:	Page 55

Steve & Christie Curtiss Collection

MARTINEZ (PACHECO)

X L C R SODA WORKS

Face:	**X L C R**
Vertical:	**SODA (Shield with star) WORKS**
Reverse:	Blank
Bottom:	**M. B.**
Color:	Aqua
Circa:	1882 - 1887
Locality:	Martinez, Cal. Contra Costa Co.
Rarity:	Common
Value:	$_____
Markota:	Page 147

The Excelsior Soda Works was established March 1882 in the town of Pacheco near Martinez by Martin Bonzagni & Raymond Angelo.

In 1887 Angelo left the bottling works and sold hay while Bonzagni relocated the bottling works to Martinez. Bonzagni closed the soda works in 1896 and went into the saloon business.

Steve & Christie Curtiss Collection

MARTINEZ

X. L. C. R. SODA WORKS MARTINEZ

Face: X L C R
Vertical: SODA (Shield with star) WORKS
                              MARTINEZ
Reverse: Blank
Bottom: M. B.
Color: Aqua
Circa: 1887 - 1896
Locality: Martinez, Cal. Contra Costa Co.
Rarity: Common
Value: $_____
Markota: Page 147

It is possible that Bonzagni used the above bottle after the move to Martinez.

Left - John Burton Collection
Right – Steve & Christie Curtiss Collection

MAYFIELD (PALO ALTO)

MAYFIELD SODA WORKS

Face: MAYFIELD
                              SODA WORKS
Reverse: Blank
Reverse: Blank
Color: Aqua
Circa: 1897 – 1902
Location: Palo Alto, Cal.
Rarity: Rare
Value: $_____
Markota: Page 79

Joseph & Lara Jacobs manufactured soda water and carbonated beverages until 1902. Anthony Martin was involved from 1897 to 1900.

Mayfield was incorporated into Palo Alto in Santa Clara County.

John Burton Collection

MELROSE

MELROSE BOTTLING WORKS

Face: MELROSE
          BOTTLING WORKS
          J. PRIMUS
Reverse: Blank
Bottom: Blank
Color: Aqua
Circa: 1885 – 1908
Locality: Annexed to West Oakland
Rarity: Extremely Rare
Value: $_____
Markota: Page 80

Primus manufactured soda water and various types of carbonated drinks. Melrose was annexed in 1908 to West Oakland.

MENDOCINO

MENDOCINO BOTTLING WORKS

Face: MENDOCINO
          BOTTLING WORKS
          A. L. REYNOLDS
Reverse: Blank
Bottom: Blank
Color: Aqua
Circa: 1905 – 1910
Locality: Mendocino County, Cal.
Rarity: Semi Rare
Value: $_____
Markota: Page 81

Reynolds purchased the bottling works from George H. Bowman in 1905 bottling until 1910. His main competitor was Ocean View Bottling Works owned by Nelson & Barry.

Steve & Christie Curtiss Collection

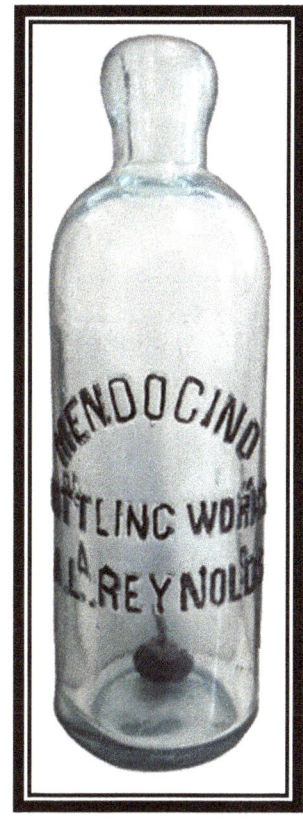

John Burton Collection

MENDOCINO
OCEAN VIEW BOTTLING WORKS

Face:	OCEAN VIEW BOTTLING WORKS N & B PROPS. MENDOCINO, CAL.
Reverse:	Blank
Bottom:	Blank or P.C.G.W.
Base:	Different shaped bases
Color:	Aqua
Circa:	1905 – 1914
Locality:	Mendocino, Cal. Mendocino Co.
Rarity:	Semi Rare
Value:	$_____
Markota:	Page 95

Nelson & Barry manufactured and distributed various sodas, syrups and cider in Mendocino. They closed the plant in 1914

MILLS
MILLS' SELTZER SPRINGS

Face:	MILLS' SELTZER SPRINGS
Reverse:	Blank
Bottom:	Blank
Color:	Aqua & Light Lime Green
Circa:	1874 – 1895
Locality:	Santa Clara County
Rarity:	Extremely Rare
Value:	$_____
Markota:	Page 81

In 1869 because of ill health Luther Mills came to Santa Clara County and purchased the Congress Springs Hotel selling it in 1874. He purchased Seltzer Aperient Springs in Santa Clara Township naming it Mills Pacific Seltzer bottling mineral water & Sarsaparilla. Mills sold the springs to John Ryland who renamed the springs to Azule Seltzer Springs.

John Burton Collection

Steve & Christie Curtiss Collection

MODESTO

STANISLAUS SODA WORKS

Face:	STANISLAUS SODA WORKS MODESTO, CAL.
Reverse:	Blank
Bottom:	Blank
Color:	Aqua
Circa:	1884 – 1896
Locality:	Modesto, Cal.
Rarity:	Extremely Rare
Value:	$_____
Markota:	Page 131

Christian Brown purchased two lots on the corner of Tenth & F Streets in 1884 operating the Stanislaus Soda Works by himself until 1891 when N. C. Nelson became a partner. Brown sold the soda works in 1892 to G. W. Russ & Henry Carstens both former owners of Amador County Soda Works in Jackson. Late 1893 they sold to Hans Jacobsen & Peter Jorgensen changing the name to Modesto Soda Works.

Steve & Christie Curtiss Collection

MOKELUMNE HILL

MOK. HILL SODA WORKS

Face:	C. A. WERLE MOK. HILL
Reverse:	Blank
Bottom:	Large M
Color:	Aqua
Circa:	1876 – 1909
Locality:	Mokelumne Hill, Calaveras Co.
Rarity:	Scarce
Value:	$_____
Markota:	Page 142

Henry J. Newman & Frank Drake established the first soda works in Mokelumne in 1858. In 1874 Charles Werle purchased the soda works located on Lafayette Street from Newman. In 1876 the soda works was renamed Pioneer Soda Factory producing 50,000 bottles a month. In 1909 Werle sold to Herman & Dorothy Maasberg who renamed it Mokelumne Hills Soda Works.

John Burton Collection

MOKELUMNE HILL

MOKELUMNE HILL SODA WORKS

Face:	MOKELUMNE HILL SODA WORKS
Reverse:	Blank
Bottom:	M
Color:	Clear & Amber
Circa:	1890 - 1909
Locality:	Mokelumne Hill, Calaveras Co.
Rarity:	Scarce
Value:	$_____
Markota:	Page 82

In 1909 Werle sold to Herman & Dorothy Maasberg who renamed it Mokelumne Hills Soda Works from Pioneer Soda Factory.

John Burton Collection

MOUNTAIN VIEW

GOLDEN WEST SODA WORKS

Face:	GOLDEN WEST SODA WORKS BRUNS & NASH MOUNTAIN VIEW CAL.
Reverse:	Blank
Bottom:	Blank
Color:	Clear & Amber
Circa:	1893 - 1910
Locality:	Mountain View (San Jose area)
Rarity:	Extremely Scarce
Value:	$_____
Markota:	Page 51

Steve & Christie Curtiss Collection

MONTEREY

MONTEREY SODA WORKS

Face:	PROPERTY OF MONTEREY SODA WORKS CAL.
Reverse:	Blank
Bottom:	51/B
Color:	Aqua
Circa:	1890 – 1915
Locality:	Monterey, Cal.
Rarity:	Scarce
Value:	$_____
Markota:	Page 107

John R. Kennedy started the Monterey Soda Works around 1890 on Pacific Street manufacturing and distributing soda water until about 1903.

In 1903 A. L. Weaver purchased the soda works and sold it in 1907 to W. T. Read who operated it until 1915.

John Burton Collection

MONTEREY

MONTEREY SODA WORKS

Face:	MONTEREY SODA WORKS CAL.
Reverse:	Blank
Bottom:	Blank
Color:	Aqua
Circa:	1890 – 1915
Locality:	Monterey, Cal.
Rarity:	Scarce
Value:	$_____
Markota:	Unlisted

Bottle was found in the ocean with sea shells growing inside bottle

Steve & Christie Curtiss Collection

MONTEREY
MONTEREY BOTTLING WORKS

Face:	MONTEREY BOTTLING WORKS
Reverse:	Blank
Bottom:	Blank
Color:	Aqua
Circa:	1890 – 1915
Locality:	Monterey, Cal.
Rarity:	Scarce
Value:	$_____
Markota:	Page 107

Steve & Christie Curtiss Collection

MONTEREY
ENTERPRISE SODA WATER COMPANY

Face:	ENTERPRISE SODA WATER CO. MONTEREY
Reverse:	Blank
Bottom:	Blank or 329H or 429H
Color:	Aqua
Circa:	1905 – 1920
Locality:	Monterey, Cal.
Rarity:	Extremely Rare
Value:	$_____
Markota:	Page 43

In 1905 Charles D. Casper and & his wife were proprietors of Enterprise Soda Water Company at 1428 Tyler Street. Casper also operated the Casper Hotel and had a contracting business. They sold the soda water company to J. J. Fenton in 1915 who operated the business into the mid-1920's.

John Burton Collection

NAPA

ED HENRY SODA
Face: ED HENRY
                  Monogram E H
                  NAPA, CAL.
Reverse: Blank
Bottom: Blank
Color: Aqua
Circa: 1901 – 1919
Locality: Napa, Cal.
Rarity: Semi Common
Value: $_____
Markota Page 60

Ed Henry was an agent for Jackson's Napa Soda Water. His early Blob Top bottles have his name embossed on the reverse. Henry was also a dealer in wines & liquor's as well as manufacturing soda water. He was a member of the Napa City Council.

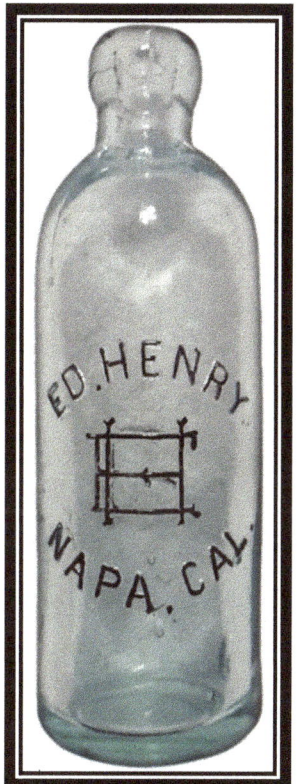

John Louder Collection

NAPA

LUDWIG SODA MANUFACTURER
Face: A. LUDWIG
                  NAPA
                  CAL.
Reverse: Blank
Bottom: Blank or P.C.G.W.
Color: Aqua
Circa: 1900 – 1908
Locality: Napa, Cal.
Rarity: Semi Common
Value: $_____
Markota: Page 75

Owner of the Golden Edge Saloon he started manufacturing soda water around 1900 until 1908.

John Burton Collection

NAPA

LUDWIG SODA MANUFACTURER

Face: A. LUDWIG
                NAPA
Reverse: Blank
Bottom: Blank or P.C.G.W.
Color: Aqua
Circa: 1900 – 1908
Locality: Napa, Cal.
Rarity: Semi Common
Value: $_____
Markota: Page 75

Ludwig was also the owner of Vichy Springs Soda works from 1910 to 1913

P. C. G. W. stands for Pacific Coast Glass Works company located in San Francisco.

John Burton Collection

NAPA

WALTERS NAPA

Face: WALTER'S
                NAPA
                COUNTY
                SODA
                HUTCHINS
                &
                REYNOLDS
Reverse: Blank
Bottom: Blank
Color: Aqua
Circa: 1910
Rarity: Semi Common
Value: $_____
Markota: Unlisted

Walters Spring's Napa. Believe that Reynold's had been with Mendocino Bottling Works.

John Burton Collection

NEVADA CITY

STAR SODA WORKS

Face:	STAR SODA WORKS
	Monogram STAR
	GRIBBLE & Co.
	NEVADA, CITY
Reverse:	Blank
Bottom:	Blank
Color:	Aqua
Circa:	1899 – 1903
Locality	Nevada City – Grass Valley
Rarity:	Rare
Value:	$_____
Markota:	Page 131

James Thomas Gibble proprietor of the Star Soda Works competing against Daniel & Powell who were also located in Nevada City.

Can't find any information regarding Daniel & Powell.

Steve & Christie Curtiss Collection

NEVADA CITY

NEVADA CITY SODA WORKS (Vertical)

Face:	NEVADA CITY SODA WORKS
	E. T. R. POWELL
Reverse:	Blank
Bottom:	Blank
Color:	Aqua
Circa:	1904 – 1920
Locality:	Nevada City, Ca.
Rarity:	Scarce
Value:	$_____
Markota:	page 88

Steve & Christie Curtiss Collection

NEVADA CITY

NEVADA CITY SODA WORKS

Face:	NEVADA CITY SODA WORKS (Flower) E. T. R. POWELL
Reverse:	(Vertical) NEVADA CITY SODA WORKS E. T. R. POWELL
Bottom:	Blank
Color:	Aqua
Circa:	1904 - 1910
Locality:	Nevada City, Ca.
Rarity:	Extremely Rare
Value:	$_____
Markota:	Page 88

(Edward Thomas Robert Powell)

John Baugh, James L. Bonney & E.T.R. Powell were listed as soda manufacturers of soda water, sarsaparilla, Iron, cider, & ginger ale in the early 1890's. Also listed as agents for Fredericksburg Beer.

Baugh left the company in 1892 and the company was known as Bonney & Powell until 1895 when Bonney left and William H. Daniel became Powell's partner. The new partnership added mineral water, champagne cider, celery, orange soda and Buffalo Beer to their portfolio.

William Daniel apparently died in 1904 and Powell continued to operate the business located on the corner of Spring & Pine streets into the 1920's.

Steve & Christie Curtiss Collection

John Burton Collection

OAKLAND
J. I. BLIVENS & Co.

Face:	J. I. BLIVENS & Co. OAKLAND CAL.
Reverse:	Blank
Bottom:	GRAVITATING STOPPER MADE BY JOHN MATTHEWS PAT. OCT. 11, 1864 NEW YORK
Color:	Aqua & Lime Green
Circa:	1872 – 1880
Locality:	Oakland, Cal.
Rarity:	Aqua Scarce Lime Green Extremely Rare
Value	$_____ Aqua $_____ Lime Green
Markota:	Page 16

Blivens, a former partner with Bay City Soda Works & California Axel Grease in San Francisco, started Pioneer Soda Works at 655 Broadway in Oakland. He moved to 13th & Franklin in 1877 and John D. Taylor became a partner. In 1880 Paul Lohse joined Taylor as a partner.

John Burton Collection

OAKLAND
JOHN D. TAYLOR PIONEER SODA WORKS

Face:	JOHN D. TAYLOR & Co. PIONEER SODA WATER WORKS OAKLAND * CAL.
Reverse:	Blank
Bottom:	GRAVITATING STOPPER MADE BY JOHN MATTHEWS PAT. OCT.11, 1864 NEW YORK
Variant:	Some bottles without Star
Locality:	Oakland, Cal.
Rarity:	Scarce
Value:	$_____
Markota:	Page 134

Paul Lohse left the soda works and Taylor continued to operate it until the incorporation in 1895.

Steve & Christie Curtiss Collection

OAKLAND

TAYLOR & LOHSE

Face: **TAYLOR & LOHSE SUCCESSORS TO J. I. BLIVENS & Co. OAKLAND CAL.**
Reverse: Blank
Bottom: **GRAVITATING STOPPER MADE BY JOHN MATTHEWS PAT. OCT.11, 1864 NEW YORK**
Color: Aqua & Lime Green
Circa: 1872 – 1880
Locality: Oakland, Cal.
Rarity: Aqua Scarce
Lime Green Extremely Rare
Value: $_____ Aqua
$_____ Lime Green
Markota: Page 135

Steve & Christie Curtiss Collection

OAKLAND

OAKLAND PIONEER SODA WATER

Face: **OAKLAND PIONEER CO. SODA WATER**
Reverse: Blank
Bottom: Blank
Color: Aqua
Circa: 1895 – 1933
Locality: Oakland, Cal.
Rarity: Extremely Rare
Value: $_____
Markota: Page 94

Proprietor John Taylor started this company and merged Oakland Soda Works and The Distilled Soda Water Company.

Steve & Christie Curtiss Connection

OAKLAND
THE DISTILLED SODA WATER COMPANY

Face: THE DISTILLED SODA WATER Co.
FIFTH &
KIRKHAM STs.
OAKLAND

Reverse: Blank
Bottom: Blank
Color: Aqua
Circa: 1892 – 1896
Locality: Oakland, Cal.
Rarity: Rare
Value: $_____
Markota: Page 36

Walter J. Scott & George N. Tichenor were located on the corner of Fifth & Kirkham Streets. In 1894 Abel W. Baker Jr. replaced Tichenor as secretary treasurer.

In 1896 the Distilled Soda Water company, Pioneer Soda Works & Oakland Soda Works incorporated forming the Oakland Pioneer Soda Water Company.

Steve & Christie Curtiss Collection

OAKLAND
OAKLAND PIONEER SODA WATER COMPANY

O. P. S. W. Co.
Monogram: Bottle in circle of Trade Mark
REGISTERED
BOTTLE IS NEVER SOLD

Reverse: Blank
Bottom: Blank
Color: Aqua
Circa: 1895 – 1933
Locality: Oakland, Cal.
Rarity: Scarce
Value: $_____
Markota: Page 97

Oakland Pioneer Soda Works was located at 343 Tenth Street and moving to 13th & Webster Streets. In 1913 the name was changed to Pioneer Beverage Company.

Steve & Christie Curtiss Collection

OAKLAND
OAKLAND PIONEER SODA WATER COMPANY

Face:	OAKLAND PIONEER
Monogram:	Bottle in circle of Trade Mark
	SODA WATER CO.
	BOTTLE IS NEVER SOLD
Reverse:	Blank
Bottom:	Blank
Color:	Aqua
Circa:	1895 – 1933
Locality:	Oakland, Cal.
Rarity:	Scarce
Value:	$_____
Markota:	Page 94

Oakland Pioneer Soda Works, Oakland Soda Works, & The Distilled Soda Water Companies incorporated in 1895 becoming Oakland Pioneer Soda Company. John Taylor of the Pioneer Soda Works became president, William Lang of Oakland Soda Works vice-president & Abel Baker Jr. of Distilled Soda Water Company secretary.

Steve & Christie Curtiss Collection

OAKLAND
OAKLAND SODA WORKS

Face:	OAKLAND
	LM
	SODA WORKS
Reverse:	Blank
Bottom:	+
Color:	Aqua
Circa:	1894 - 1895
Locality:	Oakland, Cal.
Rarity:	Rare
Value:	$_____
Markota:	Page 95

William Lang, former manager of Lang Brothers Beer Bottlers in Oakland with Jacob Many located at 221 -223 8th Street in Oakland.

Short lived, William Lang became vice-president of the new consolidation, Oakland Pioneer Company.

Steve & Christie Curtiss Collection

OAKLAND

      OAKLAND STEAM SODA WORKS

Face:	OAKLAND
Monogram:	SUN image
	STEAM SODA WORKS
	BOTTLE IS NOT TO BE SOLD
Reverse:	Blank
Bottom:	Blank
Base:	THIS BOTTLE IS NOT SOLD
Color:	Aqua
Circa:	1889 – 1908
Locality:	Oakland, Cal.
Rarity:	Semi Rare
Value:	$_____
Markota:	Page 93

Established by David D. Montgomery as president, Jacob Many vice-president & Julius Somps manage at 1628 Grove Street. Agents for Lytton Geyser and Vichy water until 1902 when all three went back to work for their previous employer the Oakland Pioneer Soda Water Company.

John Burton Collection

OAKLAND

      SILVER STILL PURE WATER CO.

Face:	SILVER STILL
	PURE WATER CO.
	OAKLAND
Reverse:	Blank
Bottom:	+
Color:	Aqua
Circa:	1904 – 1907
Locality:	Oakland. Cal.
Rarity:	Rare
Value:	$_____
Markota:	Page 126

Founded in 1900 by Henry H. Linnell at 1930 Haste Street in Berkeley moving to Oakland in 1904. Now located on the corner of Lowell & Grace Streets moving in 1905 to corner Lowell & Stanford Streets. He closed the doors in 1907 becoming a traveling salesman.

Steve & Christie Curtiss Collection

OAKLAND
OAKLAND BOTTLING CO.

Face:	OAKLAND BOTTLING CO.
Reverse:	Blank
Bottom:	Blank
Color:	Aqua
Circa:	1892 -1908
Locality:	Oakland. Cal.
Rarity:	Rare
Value:	$_____
Markota:	Unlisted

Established by Frederick & Joseph Stromberg, Frank Ahren & Charle Franck. Located at `4`9 Broadway between 19th and 20th Streets.

Ahren inherited the company in 1903 And Carl S. Plant became manager until 1907 with John Heaney taking over.

Steve & Christie Curtiss Collection

OAKLAND
ALAMEDA SODA WATER Co.

Face:	ALAMEDA
	(Hands Shaking)
	SODA WATER CO.
	OAKLAND, CAL.
	BOTTLE IS NOT SOLD
Reverse:	Blank
Bottom:	Blank
Color:	Aqua
Circa:	1898 - 1902
Locality:	Alameda, Oakland. Cal.
Rarity:	Extremely Rare
Value:	$_____
Markota:	Page 3

Thomas Lund & Lot Moore. Main facility was in San Francisco. Alameda plant was located at 2303 Buena Vista Avenue in Alameda.

Steve & Christie Curtiss Collection

OROVILLE

	E. HIGGINS
Face:	Blank
Reverse:	Blank
Bottom:	E. HIGGINS OROVILLE
Color:	Aqua
Circa:	1875 – 1887
Locality:	Oroville, Cal. Butte County
Rarity:	Common
Value:	$_____
Markota:	Page 61

Edward Higgins stared the Oroville Soda Works around 1875 until 1887 located on Montgomery Street.

He manufactured carbonated soda, and delt in retailing Mt.Ida Mineral Water.

John Burton Collection

OCCIDENTAL

	OCCIDENTAL BOTTLING WORKS
Face:	OCCIDENTAL BOTTLING WORKS
	Monogram OBW
	OCCIDENTAL, CAL.
Reverse:	Blank
Bottom:	B. P.
Color:	Aqua
Circa:	1908 – 1911
Locality:	Occidental, Cal. Sonoma County
Rarity:	Common
Value:	$_____
Markota:	Page 96

Burt C. Philbrick started the Occidental Bottling Works in 1908. Philbrick had been an employee of William H. Hudson who had a major bottling plant in Santa Rosa.

John Burton Collection

ONTARIO

O. K. SODA WORKS

Face:	O. K.
	SODA
	WORKS
Reverse:	Blank
Bottom:	Some blank or with H or 328
Color:	Aqua
Circa:	1905
Locality:	Ontario Southern Cal.
Rarity:	Very Rare
Value:	$_____

Unlisted

Eddie Kuskie Collection

OXNARD

OXNARD SODA WORKS

Face:	WOOD & BELL
	OXNARD, CAL.
Reverse:	Blank
Bottom:	Blank
Color:	Aqua
Circa:	1905
Locality:	Ontario Southern Cal.
Rarity:	Unique
Value:	$_____

Unlisted

Steve & Christie Curtiss Collection

PASADENA

THE IMPROVED SODA WORKS

Face:	THE IMPROVED SODA WORKS PASADENA
Reverse:	Blank
Bottom:	Blank
Color:	Aqua
Circa:	1890 – 1905
Locality:	Pasadena, Cal. Los Angeles Co.
Rarity:	Rare
Value:	$_____
Markota:	Page 136

NOT A TORNADO BUT HEAVY WINDS

The building of the Pasadena Soda Works building owned by H. W. Stoll was blown down and superintendent Mr. Gamshauser was asleep at the time. He miraculously escaped injury.

Los Angeles Herald December 12, 1891

Left – Steve & Christie Curtiss Collection
Right - Eddie Kuskie Collection

PASO ROBLES

PASO ROBLES SODA WORKS

Face:	Blank
Reverse:	Blank
Bottom:	P. R. B. Co. P. R. in circle
Color:	Aqua
Circa:	1898 – 1920
Locality:	Paso Robles
Rarity:	Extremely Rare
Value:	$_____
Markota:	Page 99

Established in 1898 by Peter Topham & Truman Brooks on the corner of 9th & Pine Street. In 1904 Truman Brooks was the sole proprietor bottling soda water and mineral water as well as selling ice.

Embossed Varient:

PASO ROBLES SODA WORKS
PASO ROBLES

Steve & Christie Curtiss Collection

PETALUMA

ENDRES & COMPANY SODA WORKS

Face: ENDRES & CO.
PETALUMA, CAL.
Reverse: Blank
Bottom: Blank
Color: Aqua
Circa: 1895 – 1903
Locality: Petaluma, Cal. Sonoma Co.
Rarity: Very Rare
Value: $_____
Markota: Page 42

John Endres purchased the soda works from Bernard F. Connolly changing the name to Capitol Soda & Bottling Works located at 725 B Street.

John McCarthy was the manager and worked for Hammermann & Jarr when they purchased the company from Louis Schmidt in 1906.

John Burton Collection

PETALUMA

CAPITAL SODA & BOTTLING WORKS

Face: CAPITAL SODA & BOTTLING WORKS
PETALUMA
CAL.
Reverse: THIS BOTTLE
NEVER SOLD
Bottom: L.S.
Color: Aqua
Circa: 1903 – 1906
Locality, Petaluma, Cal. Sonoma County
Rarity: Very Rare
Value: $_____
Markota: Page 25

Louis Schmidt acquired the soda & bottling works located on B Street from John Endres estate who had gone mad, been placed in an institution and committed suicide.

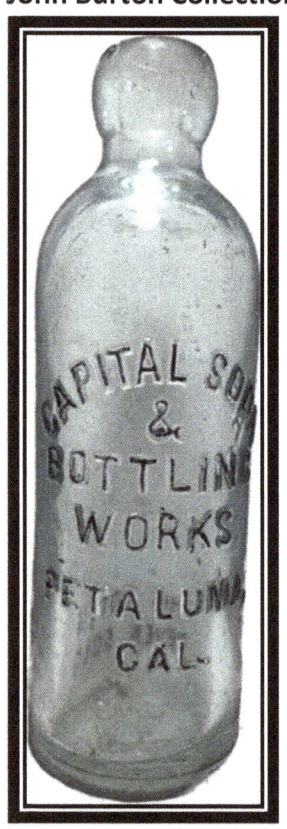

John Burton Collection

PETALUMA
CAPITAL BOTTLING WORKS

Face:	CAPITAL BOTTLING WORKS
	L.S.
	PETALUMA, CAL.
Reverse:	Blank
Bottom:	P.C.G.W.
Color:	Aqua
Circa:	1906 - 1907
Locality,	Petaluma, Cal. Sonoma County
Rarity:	Rare
Value:	$_____
Markota:	Page 24

Now located at 329 Upham Street Schmidt sold to Henry Hammermann & Johannes Jarr in 1907.

John Burton Collection

PETALUMA
HAMMERMANN & JARR SODA & SELTZER WORKS

Face:	Paper Label
Reverse:	Blank
Bottom:	M.B.W.
Color:	Aqua
Circa:	1908 – 1920's

Hammermann & Jarr changed the name to Petaluma Soda & Seltzer Works. They continued to manufacture carbonated drinks under the name Petaluma Soda & Seltzer Works with a paper label.

They also were bottlers of Wunder Lager & Steam Beer, agents for Jackson's Napa Soda water, Quir's Seltzer Water and other brands of mineral water.

Company sold to Coca Cola in the 1920's.

John Burton Collection

PETALUMA

G. W. EPLER SODA WATER

Face:	G. W. EPLER
Reverse:	Blank
Bottom:	E
Color:	Aqua
Circa:	1883
Locality:	Currently Petaluma
Rarity:	Semi common
Value:	$_____
Markota:	Page 44

This man got around. Recently run out of Oregon, stopping in Ukiah in 1881 on north State Street selling the plant to William H. Hudson of Santa Rosa Bottling Works in 1882, having a quick stop in Petaluma, then Epler opened a soda water company in Walla Walla Washington, in 1884 until 1888, purchased the Capitol Soda Works in Salem Oregon April 1892 selling June 1892 to George Collins & Lewis Gordon.

John Burton Collection

PLACERVILLE

PEARSON'S SODA WORKS

Face:	PEARSON'S SODA WORKS Both Large & Small Print Small Print Arched Large Print Straight
Reverse:	Blank
Bottom:	122 B
Color:	Aqua
Circa:	1892-1902
Locality:	Placerville, Cal.
Rarity:	Semi common
Value:	$_____
Markota:	Page 101

Steve & Christie Curtiss Collection

PLACERVILLE

PEARSON BROS. PLACERVILLE

Face:	PEARSON BROS. PLACERVILLE
Reverse:	P
Bottom:	Blank
Color:	Aqua
Circa:	1852 – 1891
Locality:	Placerville, Cal.
Rarity:	Rare
Value:	$_____
Markota:	Page 100

John McFarland Pearson started the Pearson Soda Works on Main Street near the Cedar Ravine Bridge in 1852 with his brother William. They were wholesale liquor merchants and manufactured ginger ale, bitters, syrups, peppermint and bottled English Ale, Porter, Cider as well as soda water.

Late 1850's they were also confectioners in San Francisco located at 126 Kearny Street. In the 1860's to mid-1870's the also had a soda & liquor business in Carson City Nevada as well as Bodie California in the 1880's.

After John McFarland died his son John Jr. continued the business adding distribution of beer, wine, cider & liquor.

PLACERVILLE

PEARSON SODA WORKS

Face:	P
Reverse:	P Blocked out
Bottom:	Blank
Color:	Aqua
Circa:	1852 – 1891
Locality:	Placerville, Cal.
Rarity:	Rare
Value:	$_____
Markota:	Page 100

Bottle shown here is probably from 1880 to 1910. Pearson also bottled in Bodie California.

Steve & Christie Curtiss Collection

Steve & Christie Curtiss Collection

PLYMOUTH
PLYMOUTH SODA WORKS

Face: PLYMOUTH
                CAL.
              SODA WORKS

Reverse: Blank
Bottom: Image of square
Color: Aqua
Circa: 1900 – 1910
Locality: Probably bottled in Jackson, Cal
Rarity: Rare
Value: $_____
Markota: Page 105

T. K. Norman, proprietor of the Jackson Soda works, lived in Plymouth with his family. An educated guess is that if he lived in Plymouth and there was no soda works factory, he could have manufactured soda in Jackson at his plant and bottled the water under the Plymouth name.

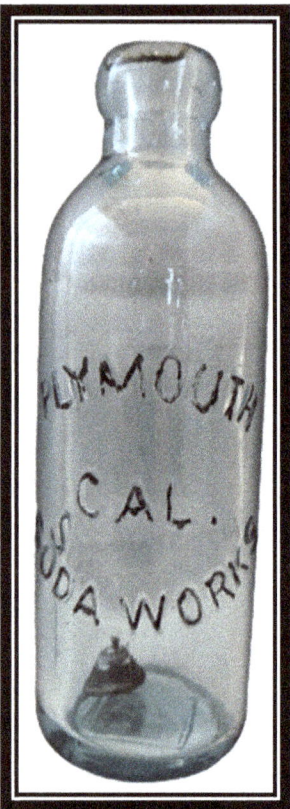

John Burton Collection

PLYMOUTH
CHAMPION SODA WORKS

Face: CHAMPION
              SODA WORKS
              PLYMOUTH, CAL.

Reverse: Blank
Bottom: Blank
Locality: Probably bottled in Jackson, Cal
Rarity: Rare
Value: $_____
Markota: Page 28

Frank Podesta and Henry Tallon formed their partnership March 30, 1900 3stablishing a soda works located in the Sanguinetti building on North Street. They dissolved their partnership in September 1900. In 1903 Podesta purchased the Reichlng residence moving the soda works and his saloon next to his residence.

In August 1909 T. K. Norman purchased the soda works of Podesta & Gambo according to the Amador Ledger-Dispatch.

Steve & Christie Curtiss Collection

POMONA

	POMONA SODA WORKS
Face:	POMONA
	SODA WORKS
	POMONA, CAL.
Reverse:	THIS BOTTLE NOT TO BE SOLD
Bottom:	Blank
Color:	Pale Green Aqua
Circa:	1895 - 1910
Locality:	Pomona, Cal. Los Angeles, Co.
Rarity:	Extremely Rare
Value:	$_____
Markota	Page 105

John Weber proprietor of the Pomona Soda Works and agent for Union Ice Company was located on North Main between 1st & Bertie Streets.

Bottle is a two-piece mold with wide top and embossed in a slug plate sealed with a wooden ball.

Steve & Christie Curtiss Collection

POMONA

	POMONA SODA WORKS
Face:	POMONA
	SODA WORKS
	POMONA, CAL.
Reverse:	THIS BOTTLE NOT TO BE SOLD
Bottom:	P. C. G. W.
Color:	Blue Aqua
Circa:	1902 – 1910
Locality:	Pomona, Cal. Los Angeles, Co.
Rarity:	Rare
Value:	$_____
Markota	Page 105

This bottle also in a two-piece mold with a wide mouth and sealed with a wooden ball.

Steve & Christie Curtiss Collection

POINT RICHMOND

RICHMOND SODA WORKS

Face:	RICHMOND SODA WORKS R.S.W. POINT RICHMOND
Reverse:	Blank
Bottom:	Some have P. C. G. W.
Color:	Aqua
Circa:	1902 – 1915
Locality:	Point Richmond, Cal. Contra Costa, County
Rarity:	Scarce
Value:	$_____
Markota:	Page 110

Rueben Curry founded the Point Richmond Soda Works in 1902 at 932 Ohio Street corner of 10th bottling 45,000 bottles a month. In 1904 the soda works moved to 932 Ohio Street then again to 1134 Ohio Street.

In 1915 the name changed to Richmond Soda Works & Bottling Company. The company changed hands several times ending up with the original owner.

Steve & Christie Curtiss Collection

PORT COSTA

PORT COSTA SODA WORKS

Face:	J. C. PORT COSTA SODA WORKS
Reverse:	Blank
Bottom:	Blank
Color:	Aqua
Circa:	1895 – 1910
Locality:	Port Costa, Cal Contra Costa Co.
Rarity:	Rare
Value:	$_____
Markota:	Page 66

Jeremiah P. Casey owner of the Ferry Exchange boarding house, was a bar owner and established the Port Costa Brewery. He also happened to be the local Justice of the Peace & local Judge.

Steve & Christie Curtiss Collection

REDDING

	A.& K. REDDING
Face:	Blank
Reverse:	Blank
Bottom:	A. & K. / REDDING
Color:	Aqua
Locality:	Redding, Cal. Shasta County
Circa:	1880 - 1889
Rarity:	Common
Value:	$_____
Markota:	Page 1

In the early 1880's William Allen & Edward W. Kenny founded the Shasta County Soda Works on the corner of Market & North Streets. Allen and Kenny were manufacturers of soda water, champagne cider, sarsaparilla & iron tonic. Iron tonic acted as a tonic for the blood.

Allen & Kenny also were agents for the Union Ice Company and it is not known if they bottled beer, however, it was advertised that they would pay cash for beer and cider bottles. Allen left the company leaving Kenny as sole proprietor.

Steve & Christie Curtiss Collection

REDDING

	ZEIS & SONS SODA WORKS
Face:	ZEIS & SONS
	REDDING, CAL.
	BOTTLE IS NEVER SOLD
Reverse:	Blank
Bottom:	Blank
Color:	Aqua
Circa:	1897 – 1920
Locality:	Redding, Cal. Shasta County
Rarity:	Rare
Value:	$_____
Markota:	Page 148

John Zeis & sons founded the Redding Ice & Bottling Company at 701 Oregon Street manufacturing bottled soda, sarsaparilla, orange cider and all types of flavors.

John Burton Collection

REDDING

ZEIS & SONS SODA WORKS

Face: ZEIS & SONS
           REDDING, CAL.
Reverse: Blank
Bottom: Blank
Color: Aqua
Circa: 1897 – 1920
Locality: Redding, Cal. Shasta County
Rarity: Rare
Value: $_____
Markota: Page 148

They were also agents for Cook's & Upper Soda Springs, mineral waters and bottlers of Blue & Gold beer.

Steve & Christie Curtiss Collection

RED BLUFF

CIRCLE PAULSON & COMPANY

Face: CIRCLE POULSON & Co.
           RED BLUFF
           CALA.
Reverse: Blank
Bottom: GRAVITATING STOPPER MADE BY JOHN MATTHEWS PAT. OCT. 11, 1864 NEW YORK
Color: Aqua
Circa: 1880 – 1885
Locality: Red Bluff, Cal. Tehama County
Rarity: Rare
Value: $_____
Markota: Page 29

Circle Paulson & Company were short lived in Red Bluff. No information at California Digital Newspapers on-line until June 2024.

Steve & Christie Curtiss Collection

RED BLUFF

D. S. CONE SODA WORKS

Face:	D. S. CONE
	I. & R. CO.
	R. B.

I & R stood for Ice & Refrigeration.

Reverse:	Blank
Bottom:	328 H
Color:	Clear, Aqua & Sun color
Circa:	1904 – 1920
Locality:	Red Bluff, Cal. Tehama County
Rarity:	Rare
Value:	$_____
Markota:	Page 31

Douglas Spencer Cone was in the produce, livestock, wool & fruit business and ice and refrigeration business located at 1104 Monroe Street. He also was manufacturing carbonated beverages and an agent for beer, wines, and mineral waters.

John Burton Collection

RIVERSIDE

RIVERSIDE SODA WORKS

Face:	RIVERSIDE
	SODA WORKS
	Codd type bottle
Reverse:	Blank
Bottom:	P. C. G. W.
Color	Blue Aqua
Circa:	1890 -, 1920
Locality:	Riverside, Cal.
Rarity:	Extremely rare
Value:	$_____
Markota:	Page 112

F. I. Hill started the Riverside Soda works at the northeast corner of Olive, & Main near Seventh Street. In 1905 the business was sold to L. C. & P. W. Lord brothers. They bottled all types soft drinks including Royal Crown Ginger Ale into the 1920's.

Left -Steve & Christie Curtiss Collection
Right - Eddie Kuskie Collection

SACRAMENTO

WILLIAM HOLDEN'S HUB PUNCH

Face:	H
	SAC.
Reverse:	P
Bottom:	C. S. W.
	SAC.
Color:	Aqua
Circa:	1881 – 1882
Locality:	Sacramento, Cal.
Rarity:	Common
Value:	$_____
Markota:	Page 54

The H & P stands for Hub Punch that was a clear cordial mixed with water, soda water cold tea or Lemonade.

Hub Punch was based out of Boston with Richards & Harrison agents in San Francisco. Apparently, Holden was selling Hub Punch without permission.

Steve & Christie Curtiss Collection

SACRAMENTO

HOLDEN'S GINGER ALE

Face:	HOLDEN'S
	G. A.
Reverse:	Blank
Bottom:	CAPITOL SODA WORKS
	SAC.
Base:	10-Sided paneled bottle
Color:	Aqua
Circa:	1881 – 1883
Locality:	Sacramento, Cal.
Rarity:	Common
Value:	$_____
Markota:	Page 62

After William Holden's problem of pirating Hub Punch, he convinced Henry J. Postel to bottle his ginger ale. His advertisement mentioned; "Holden's Ginger Ale for sale at all saloons in town, Cheaper than Napa Soda, and bottled at the Capitol Soda Works, 308 J Street between third & Fourth Streets."

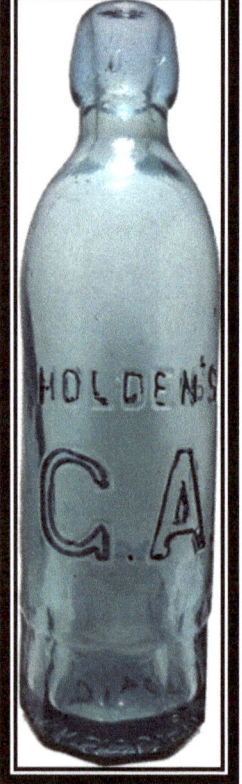

John Burton Collection

SACRAMENTO
UNION SODA WORKS

Face:	Blank (Paper Label)
Reverse:	Blank
Bottom:	U. S. W.
	SAC.
Base:	Blank
Color:	Aqua & Lime Green
Circa:	1884 - 1886
Locality:	Sacramento, Cal.
Rarity:	Rare
Value:	$_____
Markota:	Page 139

Union Soda Works located at 1920 O Street with William Holden & August Kuhn listed as proprietors.

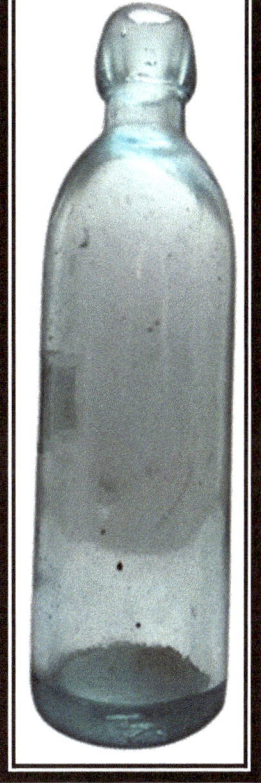

Steve & Christie Curtiss Collection

SACRAMENTO
HENRY POSTEL SODA WORKS

Face:	HENRY J. POSTEL
	SACRAMENTO
	CAL.
Reverse:	Blank
Bottom:	CAPITAL SODA WORKS
Color:	Aqua
Circa:	1881 – 1887
Locality:	Sacramento, Cal.
Rarity:	Common
Value:	$_____
Markota	Page 106

Former bookkeeper of the Columbus Brewery in 1881 started the Capital Soda Works at 303 J Street and moving to 310 J Street in 1883.

He bottled Hub Punch & Holden's Ginger Ale and soon took out a trade mark on Strawberry Dew Drops.

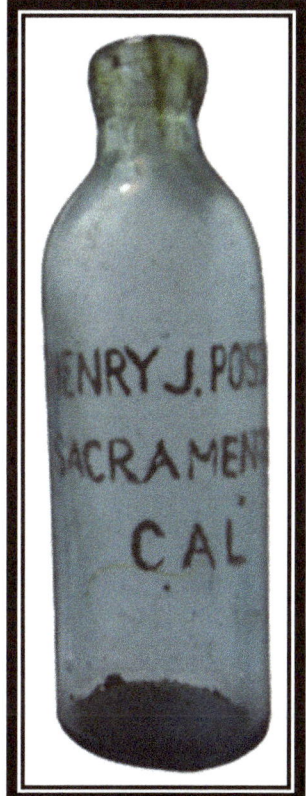

Steve & Christie Curtiss Collection

SACRAMENTO
CAPITAL SODA WORKS

Face:	**POSTEL & SCHNERR**
	SACRAMENTO
	CAL.
Reverse:	Blank
Bottom:	**CAPITAL SODA WORKS**
Color:	Aqua
Circa:	1888 – 1892
Locality:	Sacramento, Cal.
Rarity:	Common
Value:	$_____
Markota:	Page 107

Constant Schnerr joined Henry Postel as a partner of the Capital Soda Works in 1888. They moved from 310 J Street to 1111-1113 Front Street.

Now they bottled Fredericksburg beer and various brands of mineral waters. Postel retired in 1902.

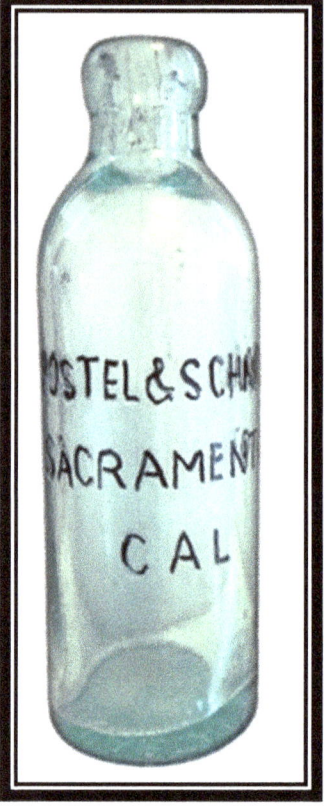

John Burton Collection

SACRAMENTO
C. SCHNERR CAPITAL SODA WORKS

Face:	**C. SCHNERR & Co.**
	SACRAMENTO
	CAL.
Reverse:	Blank
Bottom:	**CAPITAL SODA WORKS**
Color:	Clear, Aqua, Light Green & Sun
Circa:	1892 – 1908
Locality:	Sacramento, Cal.
Rarity:	Clear & Aqua common
	Light Green Rare
Value:	$_____ Clear & Aqua
	$_____ Light Green
Markota:	Page 123

After leaving Henry Postel the Schnerr brothers Constant, Edward & Antoine operated the Capital Soda Works starting in 1882. They remained at 1111-1113 Front Street bottling water until constants untimely death in 1897 Constant Jr. moved the Capital Soda Works to 310 K Street staying until 1908.

Steve & Christie Curtiss Collection

SACRAMENTO

C. SCHNERR & COMPANY

Face:	C. SCHNEER & Co.
	SACRAMENTO
	CAL.
Reverse:	NEVADA CITY SODA WORKS
	Image of FLOWER
	E. T. R. POWELL
Bottom:	CAPITAL SODA WORKS
Color:	Aqua
Circa:	1892 – 1908
Locality:	Sacramento & Nevada City
Rarity:	Extremely Rare
Value:	$_____
Markota:	Page 124

Two different company's names on this bottle. This could be a salesman's sample bottle however it is unique and expensive.

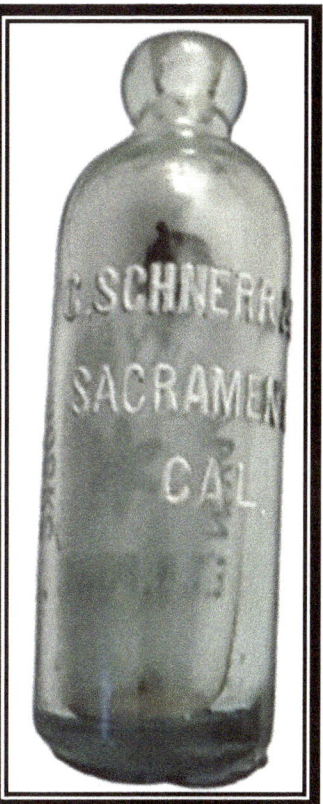

Steve & Christie Curtiss Collection

SACRAMENTO

EPHRAIM BILLINGS SODA WORKS

Face:	E. L. BILLINGS
	SACRAMENTO
	CAL.
Reverse:	Blank
Bottom:	GRAVITATING STOPPER MADE BY JOHN MATTHEWS PAT. OCT. 11, 1864 NEW YORK
Color:	Aqua
Circa:	1866 – 1883
Locality:	Sacramento, Cal.
Rarity:	Common
Value:	$_____
Markota:	Page 15

Middle of 1852 Ephraim Billings was listed as a liquor merchant, soda water manufacturer and importer of wines, liquors, dealing in brandies, agent for Geyser & Lytton soda waters. He also had a location in Folsom, California and became an agent for Jaffe's Celebrated Cinchona Bitters.

Through the years he had various partners including Owen Casey, in 1883 Billings died and his current partner, James Woodburn partnered with Barnes and the company became known as Woodburn & Barnes.

Steve & Christie Curtiss Collection

SACRAMENTO

OWEN CASEY EAGLE SODA WORKS

Face:	OWEN CASEY EAGLE SODA WORKS
Reverse:	SAC. CITY
Bottom:	Blank
Variant:	Blob Top
Color:	Aqua
Circa:	1867 -1871
Locality:	Sacramento, Cal.
Rarity:	Extremely Rare
Value:	$_____
Markota:	page 27

Owen Casey first started in 1857 as a partner with Ephraim Billings at Billings & Casey Soda Factory. In 1858 he partnered with James Kelly listed as an importer & wholesale liquor, wine & brandies and owning a soda & bottling works on K Street. They also had a soda manufactory at 54 North C Street in Carson City.

Steve & Christie Curtiss Collection

SACRAMENTO

CASEY & CRONAN EAGLE SODA WORKS

Face:	CASEY & CRONAN EAGLE SODA WORKS
Reverse:	Blank
Bottom:	GRAVITATING STOPPER MADE BY JOHN MATTHEWS PAT. OCT. 11, 1864 NEW YORK
Color:	Aqua
Circa:	1874 – 1876
Locality:	Sacramento, Cal.
Rarity:	Common
Value:	$_____
Markota:	Page 26

Owen Casey died December 15, 1871 aged 50 years. Son Hugh Casey continued the bottling works and partnered with Hugh Kelly. Late 1874 Kelley died and Casey partnered with Michael Cronan. They parted ways in 1887 and Hugh Casey stayed at 50 K Street.

John Burton Collection

SACRAMENTO
HUGH CASEY EAGLE SODA WORKS

Face:	HUGH CASEY EAGLE SODA WORKS
Reverse:	Blank
Bottom:	Blank
Color:	Aqua & Light Green
Circa:	1887 - 1905
Locality:	Sacramento, Cal.
Rarity:	Common
Value:	Clear $_____ Light Green $_____
Markota:	Page 27

Casey still located at 50 K Street until 1905 when he sold the Eagle Soda Works to his son John Casey & Edward C. Kavanaugh. Hugh Casey died December 8, 1911 age 65 years.

Steve & Christie Curtiss Collection

SACRAMENTO
HUGH CASEY EAGLE SODA WORKS

Face:	HUGH CASEY EAGLE SODA WORKS 50 K ST. SACRAMENTO CAL.
Reverse:	Blank
Bottom:	Blank
Color:	Aqua
Circa:	1887 – 1905
Locality:	Sacramento, Cal.
Rarity:	Common
Value	$_____
Markota:	Page 27

Please note that in 1880 addresses in Sacramento changed and 50 K Street became 218 K Street.

John Burton Collection

SACRAMENTO
CASEY & KAVANUGH EAGLE SODA WORKS

Face:	CASEY & KAVANAUGH TRADE MARK REGISTERED SACRAMENTO, CAL.
Reverse:	Blank
Bottom:	C & K
Color:	Aqua
Circa:	1905 – 1913
Locality:	Sacramento, Cal.
Rarity:	Rare
Value:	$_____
Markota:	Page 26

John Casey & Edward Kavanagh successors to Hugh Casey's wholesale liquor business and soda water company expanded from 118 K Street to 116-118 K Street. Around 1910 John Casey acquired a saloon & Kavanagh a barber shop at 1023 4th Street and moved their soda & wholesale business to 401 J Street. They parted ways in 1913.

John Burton Collection

SACRAMENTO
M. CRONAN SACRAMENTO

Face:	M. CRONAN 230 K STREET SACRAMENTO
Reverse:	Blank
Bottom:	Blank
Color:	Aqua
Circa:	1887 - 1897
Locality:	Sacramento, Cal.
Rarity:	Common
Value:	$_____
Markota:	Page 32

After his partnership with Hugh Casey Michael Cronan started a wholesale wine, liquor & cigar business at 230 K Street. He also bottled water at this location known as Sacramento Soda Works.

In 1898 George Wissemann joined Cronan & the business became known as Cronan and Wissemann.

John Burton Collection

SACRAMENTO

	S. C. O. H. N. M. W. ASS'N.
Face:	S. C. O. H. N. M. W. ASS'N.
	TRADE
	MARK
	REGISTERED
	SACRAMENTO, CA, CAL.
Reverse:	Blank
Bottom:	Blank
Color:	Aqua
Circa:	1902 – 1907
Locality:	Sacramento, Cal.
Rarity:	Common
Value:	$_____
Markota:	Page 125

John Haub owner of the Pabst Café on 6th Street & Martin Gastman owner of The Barrels Saloon on J Street formed a co-op bottling mineral water for members of their association. The newness or cost factor became an issue and the company dissolved in 1908.

SACRAMENTO

	S. C. O. H. N. M. W. ASS'N.
Face:	S. C. O. H. N. M. W. ASS'N.
	SACRAMENTO, CA, CAL.
Reverse:	Blank
Bottom:	Blank
Color:	Aqua
Circa:	1902 – 1907
Locality:	Sacramento, Cal.
Rarity:	Common
Value:	$_____
Markota:	Page 124

Steve & Christie Curtiss Collection

Steve & Christie Curtiss Collection

SACRAMENTO

CALIFORNIA BOTTLING WORKS

Face:
> CALIFORNIA
> BOTTLING WORKS
> T. BLAUTH
> 407 K STREET
> SACRAMANTO
> (Sacramento Misspelt)

Reverse: Blank
Bottom: Blank, P. C. G. W. or 4-Pointed Star
Color: Aqua
Circa: 1895 -1905
Locality: Sacramento, Cal.
Rarity: Rare
Value: $_____
Markota: Page 21

Theobald Blauth, a former saloon & beer hall proprietor started the California Bottling Works at 407 K Street as an agent for John Wieland's Lager Beer. He also owned a hop ranch on Freeport Boulevard.

John Burton Collection

SACRAMENTO

CALIFORNIA BOTTLING WORKS

Face:
> CALIFORNIA
> BOTTLING WORKS
> THEO. BLAUTH SONS CO.
> 407 K STREET
> SACRAMENTO

Reverse: Blank
Bottom: P. C. G. W. or 657 H or Blank
Color: Clear, Aqua & Sun Colored
Circa: 1905 -1918
Locality: Sacramento, Cal.
Rarity: Common
Value: $_____
Markota: Page 22

Theobald retired in 1905 and son's Julius & Charles continued to operate the business until 1913. Charles retired and Theobald returned to work with Julius operating the California Soda Works & wholesale liquor business until 1918.

Steve & Christie Curtiss Collection

SACRAMENTO
BERNARD McGINITY BOTTLING CO.

Face:	BERNARD McGINITY SACRAMENTO CAL.
Reverse:	Blank
Bottom:	Blank
Color:	Aqua
Circa:	1894 – 1900
Locality:	Sacramento, Cal.
Rarity:	Rare
Value:	$_____
Markota:	Page 79

McGinity was a clerk for Hugh Casey at the Eagle Soda Works, a driver and salesman for Postel & Schnerr at Capitol Soda Works.

In 1894 he started the Enterprise Soda Works at 902 Q Street until 1899 moving to 2123 Q Street for one year. In 1900 he moved to 1029 Front Street, partnered with Joseph Marty a dairy farmer for only a year. McGinity went back to work for Capitol Soda Works.

Steve & Christie Curtiss Collection

SACRAMENTO
GEORGE Z. WAIT CO.

Face:	THE GEO. Z. WAIT CARBONATING CO. SACRAMENTO, CAL. CAL.
Reverse:	Blank
Bottom:	Blank
Color:	Clear & Sun Colored
Circa:	1901 - 1928
Locality:	Sacramento, Cal.
Rarity:	Rare
Value:	$_____
Markota:	Page 140

The family name Wait started in Sacramento as early as 1860 continuing until 1928. George started in the drug store business early 1890 at 531 J Street. Water came from Fout Springs 80 miles north of Sacramento.

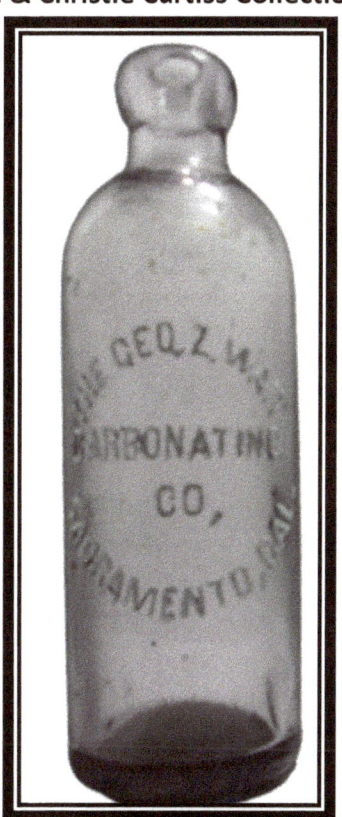

Steve & Christie Curtiss Collection

SALINAS

STEIGELMAN SODA WORKS

Face: STEIGELMAN
P.S.
SALINAS SODA WORKS

Reverse; Blank
Bottom: Blank
Color: Aqua
Circa: 1884 – 1910
Locality: Salinas, Cal. Monterey County
Rarity: Extremely Rare
Value: $_____
Markota: Unlisted

Philip Steigelman started the Salinas Soda Works on California Street near Gabilan Street.

He sold to S. Breschini & C. Molinari in 1910 who continued into the mid-1920's.

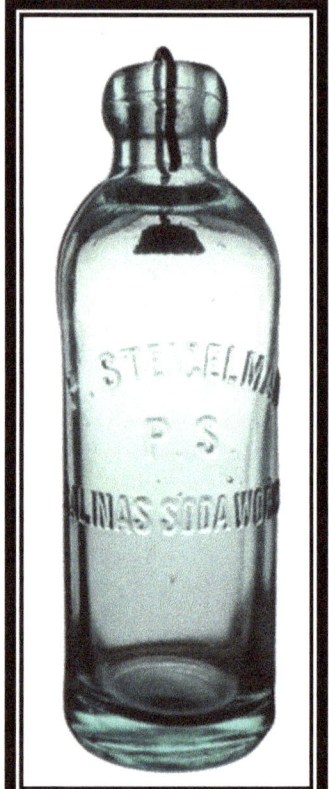

Brent Henningsen Collection

SALINAS

SALINAS SODA WORKS

Face: SALINAS
P.S.
SODA WORKS

Reverse; Blank
Bottom: Some have P. C. G. W.
Color: Aqua & Lime Green
Circa: 1884 – 1910
Locality: Salinas, Cal. Monterey County
Rarity: Rare
Value: $_____
Markota: Page 113

John Burton Collection

SAN ANSELMO

SAN ANSELMO BOTTLNG CO.

Face:	SAN ANSELMO BOTTLING CO. SAN ANSELMO, CAL.
Reverse:	Blank
Bottom:	S. A.
Color:	Aqua
Circa:	1900 – 1910
Locality:	San Anselmo, Cal.
Rarity:	Semi Rare
Value:	$_____
Markota:	Page 114

It is believed that this was a distribution point for San Anselmo Bottling Company of San Rafael, Cal.

San Anselmo was a stop for the San Rafael Branch of the North Shore Rail Road.

John Burton Collection

SAN ANSELMO

SAN ANSELMO BOTTLNG CO.

Face:	SAN ANSELMO BOTTLING CO. SAN RAFAEL, CAL.
Reverse:	Blank
Bottom:	Blank
Color:	Aqua
Circa:	1900 – 1910
Locality:	San Rafael, Cal.
Rarity:	Semi Rare
Value:	$_____
Markota:	Page 115

William Peterson was proprietor of the San Anselmo Soda Works located on D Street between Forth & Fifth Streets in San Rafael. In 1911 he was a bartender at the Luke Hotel in San Rafael.

John Burton Collection

SAN BERNARDINO
WINKLER SODA WORKS AKA CHARLES C. RILEY

Face:	AUG. WINKLER
	S.B.
	SODA WORKS
Reverse:	Blank
Bottom:	Blank
Color:	Aqua
Circa:	1883 – 1887
Locality:	San Bernadino
Rarity:	Extremely Rare
Value:	$_____
Markota:	Page 146

In 1875 August Winkler owned a saloon & bath house on Third Street. 1883 he was a liquor dealer and soda water manufacturer bottling soda until 1888 when he died in 1889. His widow sold Winkler's Soda Works to Charles C. Riley changing the name to San Bernadino Soda Works.

Winkler also operated a brewery out of the front of his bath house. His competition in the beer business was John Andreson who opened a brewery in 1880.

Steve & Christie Curtiss Collection

Eddie Kuskie Collection

SAN BERNARDINO
CITY PHARMACY SODA WORKS

Face: **BOWLAND & CRAIG CITY PHARMACY SODA WORKS SAN BERNADINE (Misspelt) CAL.**

Reverse: **GRAVITATING STOPPER MADE BY JOHN MATTHEWS PAT. OCT. 11, 1864 NEW YORK**

Bottom: Blank
Color: Aqua
Circa: 1874 – 1876
Locality: San Bernadino, Cal.
Rarity: Extremely Rare
Value: $_____
Markota: Page 18

Fielding Peters Bowland & Dr. William Craig operated the City Pharmacy Soda Works opposite the Post Office. Craig left and in 1879 Bowland is listed as proprietor of the Crystal Soda Water Factory, San Bernardino.

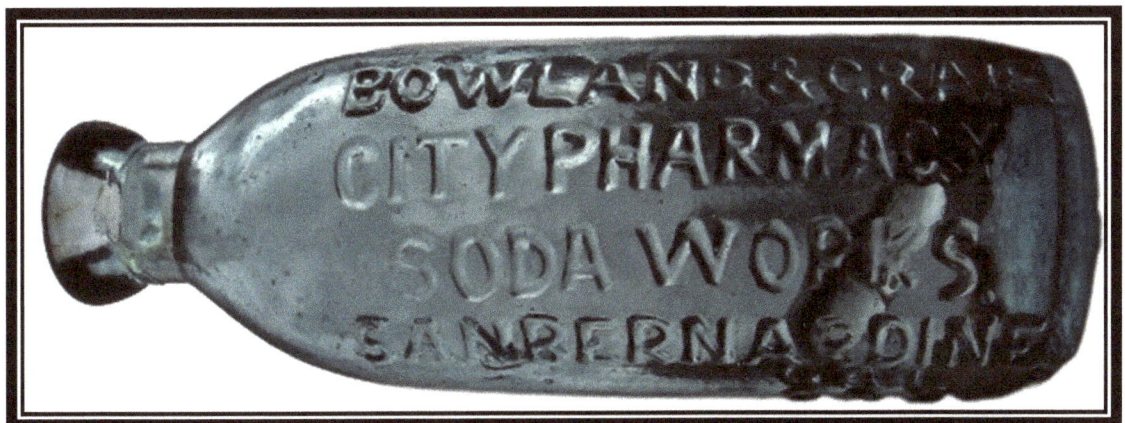

Eddie Kuskie Collection

SAN BERNADINO

C. F. RILEY SODA WORKS

Face:	C.F. RILEY
Reverse:	Blank
Bottom:	Blank
Color:	Aqua
Circa:	1880's – 1910
Location:	Eureka, San Jose & San Bernadino
Rarity:	Scarce
Value:	Aqua $_____ Blue $_____
Markota:	Page 111

Notice different tail feathers.

Left – Steve & Christie Curtiss Collection
Right - Eddie Kuskie Collection

SAN BERNARDINO

ACME SODA WORKS SAN BERNARDINO, CAL.

Face:	ACME SODA WORKS SAN BERNARDINO CAL.
Reverse:	Blank
Bottom:	S. TWITCHELL & BROTHERS Circled around FBS/S
Color:	Aqua
Locality:	Daggett, Cal. Is a guess
Circa:	1886 – 1892
Rarity:	Extremely Rare
Value:	$_____
Markota:	Page 1

Acme Soda Works was never listed as doing business in San Bernardino. With Eagle Soda Works and San Bernardino Soda Works it is believed it was bottled elsewhere. It is thought that Sheldon White bottled Acme in the town of Daggett ninety-miles away and shipped by rail to San Bernardino.

The bottle has a wide mouth with an inside indentation and was sealed by a wooden ball.

NEED PHOTO

SAN DIEGO

	X L C R SODA WORKS
Face:	XLCR
Reverse:	Blank
Bottom:	Blank
Color:	Aqua
Circa:	1881 – 1886
Locality:	San Diego, Cal.
Rarity:	Extremely Rare
Value:	$_____
Markota:	Page 147

Ferdinand J. A. Schmid founded the Excelsior Soda Works on Thirteenth Street between K & L Streets. He manufactured syrups, cider, soda, seltzers and champagne wines

Steve & Christie Curtiss Collection

SAN DIEGO

	X L C R SODA WORKS
Face:	XLCR
	SODA WORKS
Reverse:	Blank
Bottom:	Blank
Color:	Aqua
Circa:	1881 – 1886
Locality:	San Diego, Cal.
Rarity:	Extremely Rare
Value:	$_____
Markota:	Page 147

Eddie Kuskie Collection

SAN DIEGO

	X L C R SODA WORKS
Face:	F. J. A. SCHMID
	SAN DIEGO
	CAL.
	XLCR
Reverse:	Blank
Bottom:	S
Color:	Aqua
Circa:	1881 – 1886
Locality:	San Diego, Cal.
Rarity:	Extremely Rare
Value:	$_____
Markota:	Page 122

Ferdinand J. A. Schmid was also the proprietor of the Alhambra Saloon. Schmid sold the soda works to John Q. Ashton in 1887.

Steve & Christie Curtiss Collection

SAN DIEGO

	P.D. ASHTON XLCR
Face:	P. D. ASHTON
	SAN DIEGO
	CAL.
	XLCR
Reverse:	Blank
Bottom:	A
Color:	Aqua
Circa:	1887 – 1888
Locality:	San Diego, Cal.
Rarity:	Rare
Value:	$_____
Markota:	Page 7

Ferdinand J. A. Schmid owned the Excelsior Soda Works from 1881 to 1886 selling to John Q. Ashton in 1887. The soda plant was located on Thirteenth Street between K & L streets. Ashton relocated the plant to 1538 H Street. There seems to be no relation to the P. D. Ashton on the bottle other than a misprint.

Steve & Christie Curtiss Collection

SAN DIEGO

EXCELSIOR BOTTLING & EXTRACT CO.

Face:	EXCELSIOR BOTTLING AND EXTRACT CO. SAN DIEGO CAL.
Reverse:	Blank
Bottom:	Blank
Color:	Aqua
Circa:	1891 - 1903
Locality:	San Diego, Cal.
Rarity:	Scarce
Value:	$_____
Markota:	Page 46

Elijah H. Woodworth purchased the Excelsior Soda Works from John Ashton in 1891. He renamed the company to Excelsior Bottling and Extract Company. Woodworth moved to D & India Streets staying until 1903. He sold the company to Joseph Wurzell & John H. F. School who moved to 557 4th Street. They immediately sold to James Hogan who renamed it Enterprise Bottling Co.

Steve & Christie Curtiss Collection

SAN DIEGO

SAN DIEGO SODA WORKS

Face:	SAN DIEGO SODA WORKS TRADE (STAR) MARK G. GAEDKE & A. SEIFKE
Reverse:	Blank
Bottom:	Blank
Color:	Aqua
Circa:	1887 - 1888
Locality:	San Diego, Cal.
Rarity:	Rare
Value:	$_____
Markota:	Page 115

Established in 1887 by G. H. Gaedke & A. Seifke on L Street between 22nd & 23rd Streets.

Seifke left the company in 1888 and Gaedke moved to 424 Logan Avenue. Gaedke manufactured sodas, sarsaparilla, ginger ale, champagne cider & iron water, mineral water.

Steve & Christie Curtiss Collection

SAN DIEGO

	SAN DIEGO SODA WORKS
Face:	SAN DIEGO SODA WORKS
	TRADE (STAR) MARK
Reverse:	Blank
Bottom:	Blank
Base:	G. G.
Color:	Apple Green
Circa:	1888 - 1889
Locality:	San Diego, Cal.
Rarity:	Extremely Rare
Value:	$_____
Markota:	Page 115

After Seifke left the company in 1888 Gaedke revised his bottle's face with different embossing. Gaedke continued in business until 1914 when he sold to Caleb W. Hoopes, however, the deal fell through. He did sell in 1920 to Jacob L. Foerster & George F. Boehrig who moved the company to 333-335 11th Street.

Steve & Christie Curtiss Collection

SAN DIEGO

	SAN DIEGO SODA WORKS
Face:	SAN DIEGO
	TRADE (STAR) MARK
	SODA WORKS
Reverse:	Blank:
Bottom:	Blank
Base:	S. B. & G. CO.
Color:	Light Green
Circa:	1890's
Locality:	San Diego, Cal.
Rarity:	Extremely Rare
Value:	$_____
Markota:	Page 116 Number 1

Steve & Christie Curtiss Collection

SAN DIEGO

	SAN DIEGO SODA WORKS
Face:	SAN DIEGO
	TRADE (STAR) MARK
	SODA WORKS
Reverse:	Blank:
Bottom:	Blank
Color:	Aqua, Clear & Sun Color
Circa:	1889 - 1890
Locality:	San Diego, Cal.
Rarity:	Extremely Rare
Value:	$_____
Markota:	Page 116 Number 2

Steve & Christie Curtiss Collection

SAN DIEGO

	SAN DIEGO SODA WORKS
Face:	SAN DIEGO
	TRADE (STAR) MARK
	SODA WORKS
Reverse:	Blank:
Bottom:	Blank
Color:	Aqua, Clear & Sun Color
Circa:	1889 - 1890
Locality:	San Diego, Cal.
Rarity:	Rare
Value:	$_____
Markota:	Page 116 Number 3

Steve & Christie Curtiss Collection

SAN DIEGO
BRADLEY SPRING WATER CO.

Face:	BRADLEY
	SPRING WATER Co.
	Eagle in monogram
	SAN DIEGO, CAL.
Reverse:	Blank
Bottom:	P. C. G. W.
Color:	Aqua
Circa:	1897 - 1902
Locality:	San Diego, Cal.
Rarity:	Rare
Value:	$_____
Markota:	Page 18

Francis W. Bradley who owned the Santa Fe Hotel & Opera House Bar purchased the Bradley Springs near the town of Ramona. He established the Bradley Springs Water Company at 1225 C Street. Water hauled by wagon from the springs to Forest Station then by rail cars to San Diego. Around 1904 or 1905 he moved to 1058-1062 4th Street when he sold to Charles O. Richards in 1910

Both bottles branch tips up on left & down on right side. Notice long tail feathers.

Steve & Christie Curtiss Collection

Eddie Kuskie Collection

SAN DIEGO

BRADLEY SPRING WATER CO.
Face: BRADLEY
SPRING WATER Co.
Eagle in monogram
SAN DIEGO, CAL.
Different style Eagle
Reverse: Blank
Bottom: H
Color: Aqua
Circa: 1902 - 1909
Locality: San Diego, Cal.
Rarity: Rare
Value: $_____
Markota: Page 18

Charles O. Richards purchased the company in 1910 changing the name to Distilled Water & Bottling Company and moved to 8th Street northeast corner of M Street.
Notice short tail feathers.

Left – Steve & Christie Curtiss Collection
Right – Eddie Kuskie Collection

SAN FRANCISCO

AMERICAN SODA WORKS
Face: AMERICAN

SODA WORKS
S.F.
Reverse: Blank
Bottom: Blank
Color: Aqua & Lime
Locality: San Francisco
Circa: 1898 - 1915
Rarity: Rare
Value: $_____
Markota: Page 5

James J. Rooney & Ernest E. Zimmerman operated the soda works at 924 Bryant Street until the 1906 S.F. Earthquake & Fire. They relocated to 2485 Bryant Street and Peck feels that they had used blob tops until the Quake and Hutch bottles from 1907 to 1915

Steve & Christie Curtiss Collection

SAN FRANCISCO
ASTORG SPRINGS MINERAL WATER

Face: **ASTORG SPRINGS MINERAL WATER S. F. – CAL.**
Reverse: Blank
Bottom: Blank
Color: Aqua
Locality: San Francisco, Cal.
Circa: 1896 – 1906
Rarity: Scarce
Value: $_____

Alphonse Astorg owned a butcher & meat shop in San Francisco and discovered a mineral spring in Cobb Valley, Lake County. He bottled the mineral water and sold it through his meat market located at 108 Fifth Street, San Francisco.

Steve & Christie Curtiss Collection

SAN FRANCISCO
BAY CITY SODA WATER Co.

Face: Arched **BAY CITY SODA WATER Co. SAN FRANCISCO CAL.**
Reverse: Blank
Bottom: **GRAVITATING STOPPER MADE BY JOHN MATTHEWS PAT. OCT. 11, 1864 NEW YORK**
Color: Aqua
Locality: 320-322 Fell St. San Francisco
Circa: 1871 – 1913
Rarity: Semi Common
Value: $_____
Markota: Page 11

John Burton Collection

SAN FRANCISCO
BAY CITY BOTTLING WORKS

Face: BAY CITY
BOTTLING WORKS

Reverse: Blank
Bottom: BLANK
Color: Aqua
Locality: San Francisco
Circa:
Rarity: Rare
Value: $_____
Markota: Unlisted

Steve & Christie Curtiss Collection

SAN FRANCISCO
BAY CITY SODA WATER Co.

Face: Arched BAY CITY SODA WATER Co.
SAN FRANCISCO
Cal.

Reverse: Blank
Bottom: Blank
Color: Aqua
Locality: San Francisco
Circa: 1871 – 1913
Rarity: Semi Common
Value: $_____
Markota: Page 11

1871 James McEwen at 89 Stevenson Street
1879 from 116 Tyler Street to 112 Golden Gate
Avenue then to 320 Fell Street in 1907 until
1913. Assume the 1906 S. F. Earthquake and
Fire were reasons for relocating in 1906 – 1907.

Steve & Christie Curtiss Collection

SAN FRANCISCO
THE BELFAST SODA & GINGER ALE Co.

Face:	THE BELFAST SODA WATER & GINGER ALE Co. SAN FRANCISCO CAL.
Reverse:	Blank
Bottom:	B in triangle
Color:	Aqua
Circa:	1877 - 1886
Locality:	San Francisco
Rarity:	Semi Common
Value:	$_____
Markota:	Page 12

Alexander John Chambers with Thomas J. Payne were owners of Pacific Mineral Water Co. bottling Ginger Ale, English Lemonade & Soda Water at 1637 Howard Street. Chambers left in 1881 and Payne moved to 145 Valencia Street changing the name to The Belfast Ginger Ale Co. Times were difficult for Payne and he moved to a couple different locations in S.F before closing.

SAN FRANCISCO
BELFAST GINGER ALE CO.

Face:	BELFAST Trade B Mark GINGER ALE CO. S.F
Reverse:	Blank
Bottom:	Some have B in triangle
Color:	Aqua
Circa:	1888 – 1920
Locality:	Corner of Union & Octavia S. F.
Rarity:	Common
Value:	$_____
Markota:	Page 13

Frederick & Richard Steimke were located at 2769 Octavia from 1888 until 1900 then Frederick & son Deidrick with wife Anne until 1920. It appears that the Steimke's purchased the Belfast trade mark from either Payne or Chambers.

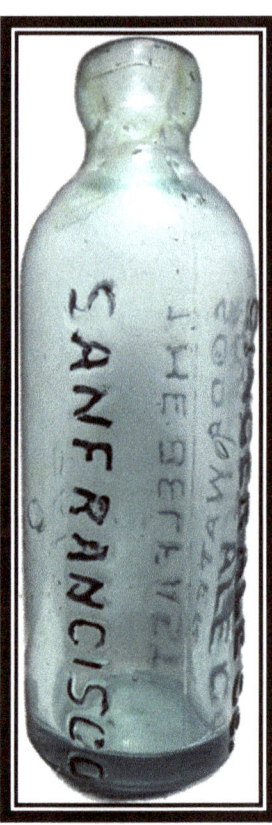

John Burton Collection

John Burton Collection

SAN FRANCISCO

BELFAST GINGER ALE CO.

Face:	**BELFAST**
	Trade **B** Mark
	GINGER ALE CO.
	S.F
Reverse:	Blank
Bottom:	Some have **B** in triangle
Color:	Aqua
Circa:	1888 – 1920
Locality:	Corner of Union & Octavia S. F.
Rarity:	Common
Value:	$_____
Markota:	Page 13

Steve & Christie Curtiss Collection

SAN FRANCISCO

BREIG & BAUER

Face:	BREIG & BAUER
	BREIG & BAUER
	S. F.
Reverse:	Blank
Bottom:	Blank
Color:	Aqua
Circa:	1890 – 1892
Locality:	San Francisco
Rarity:	Rare
Value:	$_____
Markota:	Page 19

John Breig & George Schafer operated Pacific Soda Works at 38 Hayes Street about 1879. In 1887 they moved to 1710-1712 Folsom. Schafer passed away in 1889 and Gustavus A. Bauer became a partner. Schafer's son Charles, became a partner with Breig in 1883.

Steve & Christie Curtiss Collection

SAN FRANCISCO
4 BREIG & BAUER & 3 BREIG & SCHAFER

James Quinn Collection Steve & Christie Curtiss Collection

First two James Quinn Collection Bottle 3 Steve & Christie Curtiss Collection
End bottle John Burton Collection

SAN FRANCISCO

Face:	BREIG & SCHAFER

BREIG & SCHAFER
S.F.

Reverse:	Blank
Bottom:	Blank
Color:	Aqua, Clear, Lime Green
Circa:	1891 - 1901
Locality:	San Francisco
Rarity:	Rare
Value:	$_____
Markota:	Page 20

Left _ John Burton Collection
Right - Steve & Christie Curtiss Collection

SAN FRANCISCO

Face:	BREIG & SCHAFER
	BREIG & SCHAFER

S.F.

Reverse:	Blank
Bottom:	Blank
Color:	Aqua, Clear, Lime Green, & Sun
Circa:	1891 - 1901
Locality:	San Francisco
Rarity:	Extremely Rare
Value:	$_____
Markota:	Page 20

Breig & Charles Schafer continued business at Folsom Street until 1899 moving to 1363 Harrison Street closing in 1901.

James Quinn Collection

SAN FRANCISCO
CAL. LEMONADE & SELTZER WATER CO.

Face: Arched   CAL. LEMONADE
              (Star)   CL
                      AND
            SELTZER WATER CO.
                  S.F. CAL.

Reverse:	Blank
Bottom:	Blank
Color:	Aqua
Circa:	1903 – 1917
Locality:	San Francisco
Rarity:	Extremely Rare
Value:	$_____
Markota:	Page 23

David & William C. Murdock rented a building at 172 Sanchez Street, corner 15th & Mission in 1903. William left & Daniel Leane became a partner with David. In 1913 they moved to 51 Sharon Street closing in 1917.

Steve & Christie Curtiss Collection

SAN FRANCISCO
CALIFORNIA SODA WORKS

Face: CALIFORNIA

             SODA WORKS

Reverse:	Blank
Bottom:	Blank
Color:	Aqua & Lime green
Variant:	Different size eagles
Circa:	1884 - 1898
Locality:	San Francisco
Rarity:	Common
Value:	$_____
Markota:	Page 23

Henry Goetze & Ernest Baruth opened California Soda Works in 1884 on Northeast corner Octavia & Ivy Streets. Baruth retired in 1892 selling his share to John Blohm. Goetze died in 1898 and Blohm closed the doors.

Steve & Christie Curtiss Collection

SAN FRANCISCO

CRYSTAL SODA WORKS
Face: CRYSTAL
                S. W. CO.
                S.F.
        Also comes without S. F.
Reverse: Blank
Bottom: Triangle
Color: Aqua & Lime green
Circa: 1873 - 1889
Locality: San Francisco
Rarity: Common
Value: $_____
Markota: Page 33

Sylvester R. Simmons started Crystal Soda Works in 1873 on the corner of Stockton & Union Streets. In 1875 James Daly & Frank Maxsom became partners. Having gone through different partners and moving to 2310 Mason Street the plant closed in 1889. A trade mark was taken out June 30, 1886 and that is when it is thought that they went to Hutch style bottles.

Crystal was a name used by many different bottling companies in California in different counties.

John Burton Collection

James Quinn Collection

SAN FRANCISCO
CRYSTAL SODA WATER CO.
Face: CRYSTAL
       SODA
       WATER Co.
Reverse: PATENTED
       NOV. 121872
       TAYLOR'S
       U.S. PI
Bottom: Blank
Color: Various Colors
Circa: 1873 - 1889
Locality: San Francisco
Rarity: Common
Value: $_____
Markota: Page 126

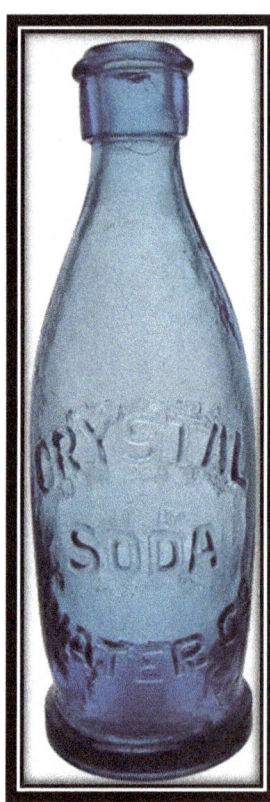

Left – John Burton Collection
Center & Right American Bottle Auctions

SAN FRANCISCO
DIAMOND SODA WORKS
Face: DIAMOND
    Trade <D> Mark
    SODA WORKS CO.
        S.F.
Reverse: Blank
Bottom: 329H and/or P.C.G.W.
Color: Aqua
Circa: 1904 - 1907
Locality: San Francisco
Rarity: Common
Value: $_____
Markota: Page 36

Located at 413 Broadway without owner mentioned. Must have been an investment company.
329H is Holt Glass Works West Berkeley in business from 1893 – 1906.
P.C.G.W. (Pacific Coast Glass Works) in business from 1902 – 1924 in San Francisco

Steve & Christie Curtiss Collection

SAN FRANCISCO
EMPIRE SODA WORKS

Face: EMPIRE SODA WORKS
SAN FRANCISCO
Reverse: FRANK
S.
WALDO

Bottom: Blank
Color: Aqua
Circa: 1880 – 1882
Locality: San Francisco
Rarity: Scarce
Value: $_____

Frank Waldo had been employed at the Belfast Ginger Ale Company to Empire Soda Works at 1721 Market Street which was also the address for Pioneer Soda Works. At the same time Waldo is also listed as proprietor of Eagle Soda Late 1882 he sold everything and moved to New York selling soda water apparatuses

 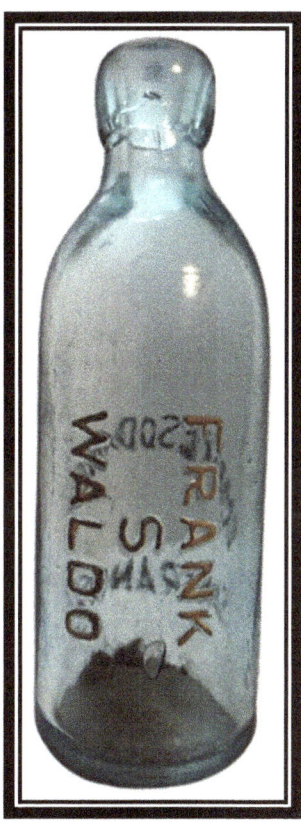

Steve & Christie Curtiss Collection

SAN FRANCISCO
EMPIRE SODA WORKS

Face: EMPIRE SODA WORKS
Reverse: FRANK
S.
WALDO & CO.

Bottom: Blank
Color: Aqua
Circa: 1880 – 1882
Locality: San Francisco
Rarity: Scarce
Value: $_____

Steve & Christie Curtiss Collection

SAN FRANCISCO
EMPIRE SODA WORKS

Waldo was involved with Empire Soda Works from 1880-1882 at 1721 Market Street, San Francisco. However, at the same time he was listed as the proprietor of Eagle Soda Works in Alameda between Oak & Park Streets.

It is belied he manufactured his San Francisco product in Alameda and used Pioneer Soda Works in San Francisco, also located at 1721 Market Street, as a warehouse and distribution location. It is believed waldo sold to Moritz Weiss and moved to New York selling soda apparatuses.

Weiss &Company information on page 2.

Steve & Christie Curtiss Collection

SAN FRANCISCO
ENTERPRISE SODA WORKS

Face:	ENTERPRISE SODA WORKS S.F. A. & W. G.
Reverse:	Blank
Bottom:	Blank
Circa:	1891 – 1894
Color:	Aqua
Locality:	San Francisco
Rarity:	Rare
Value:	$_____
Markota:	Page 44

Arthur & William Grotheen established the Enterprise Soda Works at 2735 Bryant Street bottling ginger ale, and various flavored sodas. 1894 the sold to Frederick Micheelsen and Adolph Both.

Steve & Christie Curtiss Collection

SAN FRANCISCO

	ENTERPRISE SODA WORKS
Face:	ENTERPRISE SODA WORKS S. F.
Reverse:	Some bottles have K. G. Co.
Bottom:	+
Color:	Aqua & Lime green
Circa:	1894 – 1908
Locality:	25th & Hampshire Streets S. F.
Rarity:	Extremely Rare
Value:	$_____
Markota:	Page 43

Frederick Micheelsen & Adolph Both purchased Enterprise Soda Works in 1894 located at 2725 Bryant Street from 1994 until 1890. In 1890 they moved to 1230 Hampshire Street and in 1908 changed the name to Enterprise Pioneer Bottling Works with Adolph Both & Fritz Micheelsen, Fredericks son, as owners.

Steve & Christie Curtiss Collection

SAN FRANCISCO

	ENTERPRISE SODA WORKS
Face:	Inside circle ENTERPRISE SODA WORKS S. F.
Reverse:	Some bottles have K. G. Co.
Bottom:	+
Color:	Aqua & Lime green
Circa:	1894 – 1908
Locality:	San Francisco
Rarity:	Extremely Rare
Value:	$_____
Markota:	Page 43

Adolph & Fritz closed the business in 1908. According to Markota the plant continued operation from 1909 to 1914 as Enterprise Pioneer Bottling Works and sold to Majestic Bottling Company in 1914.

Steve & Christie Curtiss Collection

SAN FRANCISCO
ENTERPRISE SODA WORKS

Face:	*E. P. S.*
	S. F.
Reverse:	Blank:
Bottom:	Blank
Color:	Aqua
Circa:	
Locality:	San Francisco
Rarity:	Extremely Rare
Value:	$_____
Markota:	Unlisted

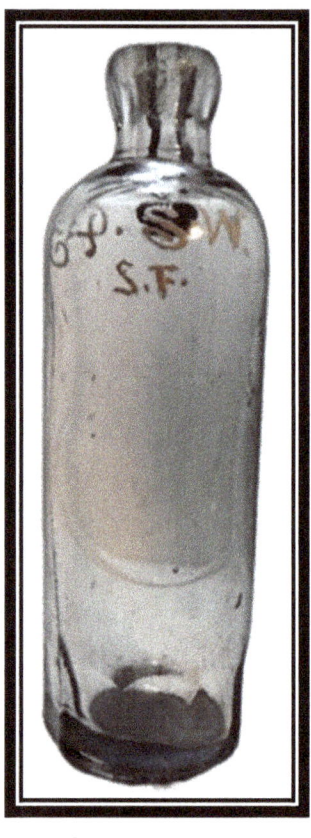

Steve & Christie Curtiss Collection

SAN FRANCISCO
EUREKA SODA WORKS

Face:	EUREKA
	SODA WORKS
	S.F.
Reverse:	Blank
Bottom:	H & H, H
Color:	Aqua
Circa:	1875 – 1884
Locality:	San Francisco
Rarity:	Rare
Value:	$_____
Markota:	Page 45

Charles Reiners & John C. Breig established Eureka Soda Works in 1872 at 541-543 Bryant moving to 723 Turk in 1874. Reiners left in 1880 and partnered with George Schafer starting Pacific Soda Works. When Reiners sold in 1884 to Louis Haake & August Hagerdorn moving to Sonoma Valley.

Steve & Christie Curtiss Collection

SAN FRANCISCO

	EUREKA SODA WORKS
Face:	EUREKA
	SODA WORKS
	S.F.
Reverse:	Blank
Bottom:	Trade Car Mark
Color:	Aqua
Circa:	1889 - 1907
Locality:	San Francisco
Rarity:	Rare
Value:	$_____
Markota:	Page 45

Around 1887 Eureka Soda Works was moved to 233 Hayes Street then in 1895 to 1756 Ellis Street. In 1898 Eureka Soda Works changed to Eureka – California Soda Water Company.

SAN FRANCISCO

EUREKA - CALIFORNIA SODA WATER COMPANY
Face: EUREKA – CALIFORNIA

                SODA WATER CO.
                      S.F.

Reverse:	Blank
Bottom:	Blank
Variant:	Different style eagles
Color:	Aqua
Circa:	1889 – 1907
Location:	San Francisco
Rarity:	Scarce
Value:	$_____
Markota:	Page 45

Incorporated in 1889 with August Hagerdorn president, John W. Goetz vice president & Louis Theirbach as secretary. First located at 1308 Turk Street until 1903 moving to 10 Briedeman Street. In 1902 Theirbach purchased Pioneer Soda Works. Majestic purchased Eureka-California Soda Water Company in 1907.

Left - Steve & Christie Curtiss Collection
Right – James Quinn Collection

Arched branch ends turn up.
Steve & Christie Curtiss Collection

SAN FRANCISCO
EUREKA - CALIFORNIA SODA WATER COMPANY
Face: EUREKA – CALIFORNIA

                SODA WATER CO.
                      S.F.

Reverse:	Blank
Bottom:	Blank
Variant:	Different style eagles
Color:	Aqua
Circa:	1889 – 1907
Location:	San Francisco
Rarity:	Scarce
Value:	$_____
Markota:	Page 45

Straight branch ends curved up
Steve & Christie Curtiss Collection

SAN FRANCISCO
EUREKA - CALIFORNIA SODA WATER COMPANY
Face: EUREKA – CALIFORNIA

                SODA WATER CO.
                      S.F.

Reverse:	Blank
Bottom:	Blank
Variant:	Different style eagles
Color:	Aqua
Circa:	1899 – 1907
Location:	San Francisco
Rarity:	Scarce
Value:	$_____
Markota:	Page 45

Branch turns both up & down
Steve & Christie Curtiss Collection

SAN FRANCISCO
EUREKA - CALIFORNIA SODA WATER COMPANY
Face: EUREKA – CALIFORNIA
                     EAGLE image
                     SODA WATER CO.

Reverse: Blank
Bottom: Blank
Color: Aqua
Circa: 1889 – 1907
Location: San Francisco
Rarity: Scarce
Value: $_____
Markota: Page 45

SAN FRANCISCO
              EUREKA SODA WORKS
Face: EUREKA
                     SODA WATERS
                      723 TURK ST.
                          S.F.
Reverse: Blank
Bottom: Blank
Color: Aqua
Circa: 1889 – 1907
Location: San Francisco
Rarity: Scarce
Value: $_____
Markota: Page 45

John Burton Collection

SAN FRANCISCO

C. A. REINERS & CO.

Face: C. A. REINERS & CO.
 723 TURK ST.
 S.F.

Reverse: Blank
Bottom: Blank
Color: Aqua
Circa: 1875 - 1884
Location: San Francisco
Rarity: Scarce
Value: $_____
Markota: Page 109

Charles A. Reiners & John C. Breig started the Eureka Soda Works at 542 -543 Bryant Street in 1874 moving later in the year to 723 Turk Street.

Breig left the company in 1880 partnering with George Schafer starting the Pacific Soda Works.

Steve & Christie Curtiss Collection

SAN FRANCISCO

FAIRMONT SODA WORKS

Face: FAIRMONT
 SODA WORKS
 S.F.

Reverse: Blank
Bottom: D. J. C.
Color: Aqua
Circa: 1901 - 1905
Locality: San Francisco
Rarity: Rare
Value: $_____
Markota: Page 48

Founded by David Curtin in 1901 located at 319 Day Street closing in 1905. Curtin left San Francisco for parts unknown.

John Burton Collection

SAN FRANCISCO
GARCIA BROTHERS

Face:	GARCIA BROS. S.F.
Reverse:	PINE-APPLE NECTAR
Bottom:	Blank
Color:	Aqua
Circa:	1882 – 1883
Locality:	San Francisco
Rarity:	Extremely rare
Value:	$_____
Markota:	Page 50

Modesto Garcia was a dealer in Havana cigars In the late 1870's to early 1880's with his brother Merardo becoming importers and dealers of fruit, cigars, & tobacco located on the Southwest corner of Washington & Sansome Streets.

Steve & Christie Curtiss Collection

SAN FRANCISCO
GLOBE MINERAL WATER

Face:	GLOBE MINERAL WATERS (Globe Image) 510 CONNECTICUT ST. S. F. BOTTLE NOT SOLD
Reverse:	Blank
Bottom:	Blank
Color:	Aqua
Circa:	1900
Locality:	San Francisco, Ca.
Rarity:	Unique
Markota:	Unlisted

Steve & Christie Curtiss Collection

SAN FRANCISCO

	HERVE & SOMPS
Face:	HERVE & SOMPS
	SAN FRANCISCO
	CAL.
Reverse:	Blank
Base:	10-sided panel
Bottom:	⌒
Color:	Aqua
Circa:	1890 – 1897
Locality:	San Francisco
Rarity:	Scarce
Value:	$_____
Markota:	Page 61

Comes both Large & Small Embossing

Eugene F. Herve & Pierre Somps started at the southwest corner of O'Farrell & Mason Streets in 1890. In 1891 they moved to 622 laguna Street and bottled various waters from Napa County until 1895. In 1897 they were listed as proprietors of Golden West Springs. It is believed that Golden West Springs was actually Walters Springs in Napa County.

SAN FRANCISCO

	SOMPS & HERVE
Face:	Small embossing
	SOMPS & HERVE
	SAN
	FRANCISCO, CAL.
Reverse:	Blank
Base:	10-sided panel
Bottom:	⌒
Color:	Aqua
Circa:	1890 – 1897
Locality:	San Francisco
Rarity:	Scarce
Value:	$_____
Markota:	Page 61

Steve & Christie Curtiss Collection

Steve & Christie Curtiss Collection

SAN FRANCISCO
PETER SOMPS SODA WORKS

Face:	P. SOMPS
	SODA WATER
	WORKS
	S. F. CAL.
Reverse:	Blank
Bottom:	Blank
Color:	Aqua
Circa:	1901-1907
Locality:	San Francisco
Rarity:	Scarce
Value:	$_____
Markota:	Page 129

Peter Somps purchased the Golden West Water Soda Works from Pierre Somps & Frank Paillet in 1901 located at 624 Laguna Street. In 1908 Peter joined Paillet as a partner in the Golden West Soda Water Works.

Steve & Christie Curtiss Collection

SAN FRANCISCO
PETER SOMPS SODA WORKS

Face:	P. S. W.
	S. F.
	Acid etched
	SODA WATER
Reverse:	Blank
Bottom:	Blank
Color:	Aqua
Circa:	1901-1907
Locality:	San Francisco
Rarity:	Extremely Rare
Value:	$_____
Markota:	Page 129

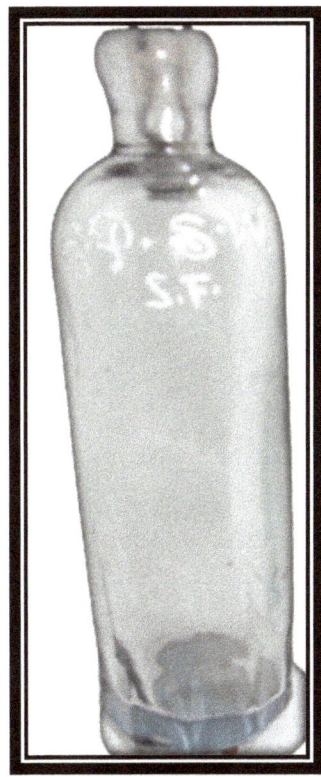

Steve & Christie Curtiss Collection

SAN FRANCISCO
GOLDEN WEST SODA WORKS

Face: GOLDEN WEST
SODA WORKS
SAN FRANCISCO
CAL.
Base: 10-Sided panel
Reverse: Blank
Bottom: (horseshoe)

Color: Aqua
Circa: 1904 – 1930
Locality: San Francisco
Rarity: Scarce
Value: $_____
Markota: Page 51

Started in 1904 by Pierre Somps & Frank Paillet at 1619-O'Farrell Street. In 1908 son Peter Somps replaced Pierre and moved to 1631 O'Farrell or there was just an address change.

John Burton Collection

SAN FRANCISCO
HERCULES MINERAL WATER

Face: HERCULES
Image of Hercules with wings
MINERAL WATER
Reverse: Blank
Bottom: C.A. M. M. in wings of a cross
Color: Aqua
Circa: 1890 – 1906
Locality: San Francisco
Rarity: Unique
Value: $_____
Markota: Page 60

Charles & Arthur Matthews bottled this mineral water at their Standard Soda Works plant located at 1134-1136 Valencia Street.

Jay Kasper Collection

SAN FRANCISCO
LIBERTY SODA WORKS

Face: LIBERTY SODA WORKS

D.W.V.S.F.

Dreyfus Wine Vaults San Francisco
Variant: Some bottles have F slugged over the S
Reverse: Blank
Bottom: CCG CO
   Cream City Glass Co. Milwaukee, Wisconsin
Color: Aqua & Light green
Circa: 1890 - 1896
Locality: San Francisco
Rarity: Scarce
Value: $_____
Markota: Page 70

Benjamin Dreyfus Company located in Europe, New York & San Francisco were dealers in California wines and brandies. They opened the Eagle wine vaults at 630-642 Brannan Street in 1881 and in 1890 started Liberty Soda Works at 511-513 Brannan Street. In 1895 they sold to Joseph Staub, John Hagler, William Reinecke & Jacob Rumetch closing in 1896.

Steve & Christie Curtiss Collection

SAN FRANCISCO
HYGEIA MINERAL WATER

Face;   HYGEIA
           MINERAL WATER Co.
           SAN FRANCISCO
           THE BOTTLE IS NOT TO BE SOLD
Reverse: Blank
Bottom: HYGEIA
Color: Aqua
Circa: 1902 – 1904
Locality: San Francisco
Rarity: Scarce
Value: $_____
Markota: Page 65

Fabian Barbanell located into the defunct Liberty Soda Works building at 3273-24th Street. Barbanell closed in 1904 moving to Los Angeles and reopening Hygeia in 1907.

John Burton Collection

SAN FRANCISCO
LYTTON SPRINGS SWEET DRINKS

Face:	LYTTON SPRINGS

	SWEET DRINKS
	P.M. H. Co.
	SAN FRANCISCO
	C.H.B.
Reverse:	Blank
Bottom:	Blank
Color:	Aqua
Circa:	1900 – 1902
Locality:	San Francisco
Rarity:	Rare
Value:	$_____
Markota:	Page 76

In 1900 Lytton Springs Water Company changed their name to Peoples Mineral – Hygiene Company lasting until 1902. The C. H. B was a misprint and should have read W. H. B. for William H. Bone president.

John Burton Collection

SAN FRANCISCO
MAJESTIC BOTTLING COMPANY

Face:	MAJESTIC BOTTLING CO. S. F.
Reverse:	Blank
Bottom:	Blank
Color:	Aqua
Circa:	1907 – 1930
Locality:	Corner Ellis & Beideman St. S. F.
Rarity:	Scarce
Value:	$_____
Markota:	Page 76

After the 1906 earthquake John W. & Edward H. Goetz of the Eureka – California Soda Water Company with Issac Spiro from the Popular Soda Water Company of which both were destroyed formed the majestic Bottling Company at 20 Biedman Street near Ellis. Hutch bottle was probably from 1907 to 1910.

Steve & Christie Curtiss Collection

SAN FRANCISCO
MANHATTAN MINERAL WATER COMPANY

Face:	MANHATTAN MINERAL WATER CO. S. F. CAL.
Reverse:	Blank
Bottom:	Blank
Color:	Aqua
Circa:	1906 – 1907
Locality:	San Francisco
Rarity:	Extremely Rare
Value:	$_____
Markota:	Page 77

Started in 1906 with limited production as it is believed the building was destroyed during the San Francisco Earthquake & Fire.

Left - Steve & Christie Curtiss Collection
Right – John Burton Collection

SAN FRANCISCO
NATIONAL SODA WORKS

Face:	NATIONAL SODA WORKS S. F.
Reverse:	Blank
Bottom:	Blank
Color:	Aqua
Circa:	1894 – 1902
Locality:	San Francisco
Rarity:	Scarce
Value:	$_____
Markota:	Page 87

Started in 1894 by Peter Svetinich and Dominic Bradasich at 525 Grove Street. In 1898 Edward Raddich became a partner staying until 1902. Svetinich and Bradasich moved to 524 Fulton Street in 1903 until 1918.

Steve & Christie Curtiss Collection

SAN FRANCISCO
NEW CENTURY STEAM SODA WORKS

Face: NEW CENTURY
           STEAM SODA WORKS
           SAN FRANCISCO
Reverse: Blank
Bottom: Some have 330 H
Color: Aqua
Circa: 1905 – 1906
Locality: San Francisco
Rarity: Rare
Value: $_____
Markota: Page 90

Giovanni Belli & Alfredo Puccinelli changed the name of New Century Soda Works to New Century Steam Soda Works for reasons unknown. Possibly "Steam" was a marketing word to improve business however the word was deleted in 1907.

Left John Burton Collection
Right Steve & Christie Curtiss Collection

SAN FRANCISCO
NEW CENTURY SODA WORKS

Face: NEW CENTURY
           SODA WORKS
           SAN FRANCISCO, CAL.
Reverse: Blank
Bottom: Some have 704
Color: Aqua
Circa: 1907
Locality: San Francisco
Rarity: Scarce
Value: $_____
Markota: Page 89

Giovanni Belli & Alfredo Puccinelli moved the operation to 3125 Laguna Street replacing Puccinelli with Ralphaelo Granucci as Belli's new partner and changing the name back to New Century Soda Works. Again, they moved this time to 436 Green Street.

Left - John Burton Collection
Right – James Quinn Collection

SAN FRANCISCO
NEW LIBERTY SODA WATER COMPANY

Face:	NEW LIBERTY
	SODA W. Co.
	Trade  Mark
	S. F.
Reverse:	Blank
Bottom:	Large +
Color:	Aqua
Circa:	1896 - 1902
Locality:	San Francisco
Rarity:	Rare
Value:	$_____
Markota:	Page 90

Founded and operated at 3272 – 24th Street by Hermann Schmidt until he died in 1901. His wife Minnie operated the soda works selling in 1902 to Fabian Barbanell who renamed it Hygenia Mineral Water Company. Not to be mistaken for Liberty Soda Works.

Steve & Christie Curtiss Collection

SAN FRANCISCO
NONPAREIL SODA WATER COMPANY

Face:	NONPAREIL
	SODA WATER CO.
	S.F.
Reverse:	Blank
Bottom:	Blank
Color:	Aqua
Circa:	1881 – 1887
Locality:	San Francisco
Rarity:	Rare
Value:	$_____
Markota:	Page 92

Samuel Benjamin listed as proprietor of Nonpareil Soda Water & Syrup Company at 719-721 Bryant Street. Prior to 1881 the location was Eastern Soda Works.

Steve & Christie Curtiss Collection

SAN FRANCISCO

PEERLESS GINGER ALE

Face:	PEERLESS GINGER ALE CO. S. F.
Reverse:	Blank
Color:	Aqua
Circa:	1903 Crocker-Langley Directory
Locality:	172 Sanchez Street S.F.
Rarity:	Extremely Rare
Value:	$_____
Markota:	Unlisted

NO INFORMATION AS OF YET

Steve & Christie Curtiss Collection

SAN FRANCISCO

PHILLIPS SODA WATER COMPANY

Face:	PHILLIPS SODA WATER Co. S.F.
Reverse:	Blank
Bottom:	Blank
Color:	Aqua
Circa:	1898 - 1901
Locality:	San Francisco
Rarity:	Extremely Rare
Value:	$_____
Markota:	Page 102

Phillips was proprietor of Phillips Napa County Soda Water Company. Prior to this he leased and managed Walter's Napa County Soda Water Company. Eventually Phillips Napa County Soda water Companies name was changed to Popular Soda Water Company operated by Samuel L. Phillips and Isaac H. Spiro in 1901.

Steve & Christie Curtiss Collection

SAN FRANCISCO
POPULAR SODA WATER COMPANY

Face:	POPULAR SODA WATER Co. S. F.
Reverse:	Blank
Bottom:	Blank
Color:	Aqua
Circa:	1901 – 1907
Locality	San Francisco
Rarity:	Scarce
Value:	$_____
Markota:	Page 106

Isaac H. Spiro purchased the Phillips Soda Water Company from Samuel Phillips in 1901 with Phillips staying on until 1902. In 1902 Spiro moved the company from 2037 15th Street to 51 Sharon Street until the 1906 earthquake. In 1907 Popular became Majestic Bottling Company.

Steve & Christie Curtiss Collection

SAN FRANCISCO
PIONEER SODA WORKS

Face:	PIONEER SODA WORKS Trade Mark (Withn "W" in shield) S. F.
Reverse:	Blank
Bottom:	Blank
Color:	Aqua
Circa:	1877 - 1896
Locality:	San Francisco
Rarity:	Common
Value:	$_____
Markota:	Page 104

Martin Walsh, Charles Welch & Raymo Angelo were proprietors in 1877 located at 1719½ Market Street moving to 1721 Market Street in 1891. Raymo Angelo left the company in 1894 and then the company was moved to 1555 Mission Street. They sold the business to William Welch and Charles Collins in 1897

Steve & Christie Curtiss Collection

SAN FRANCISCO
PIONEER SODA WORKS

Face: PIONEER
                 SODA WORKS
              Trade Mark

(Without "W" in shield)
                 S. F.

Reverse:	Blank
Bottom:	Blank
Color:	Aqua
Circa:	1877 - 1896
Locality:	San Francisco
Rarity:	Common
Value:	$_____
Markota:	Page 104

Martin Walsh, Charles Welch & Raymo Angelo were proprietors in 1877 located at 1719½ Market Street moving to 1721 Market Street in 1891. Raymo Angelo left the company in 1894 and then the company was moved to 1555 Mission Street. They sold the business to William Welch and Charles Collins in 1897

Steve & Christie Curtiss Collection

SAN FRANCISCO
PIONEER SODA WATER COMPANY

Face: PIONEER

                SODA WATER CO.
                  S.F.

Reverse:	Blank
Bottom:	Blank
Color:	Aqua
Circa:	1897 – 1906
Locality:	San Francisco
Rarity:	Extremely Rare
Value:	$_____
Markota:	Page 103

Pioneer Soda Water Company was listed at 1555 Mission Street in 1887 operated by William Welch & George Collins. In 1902 Louis Theirback assumed owner ship until 1906.

Steve & Christie Curtiss Collection

SAN FRANCISCO
G. ROTTANZI BOTTLING WORKS

Face:	G. ROTTANZI
	23D & BRYANT Sts.
	S. F.
Reverse:	Blank
Bottom:	Blank
Color:	Aqua
Circa:	1887 – 1900
Location:	San Francisco
Rarity:	Rare
Value:	$_____

Giouse Rottanzi was a dealer in foreign wines & liquors at three locations; 1027 Market Street, 1012 Valencia Street and 23rd & Bryant Street. His brother, Leopold was manager. Rottanzi manufactured Pride of California Champagne, distilled grape Brandy and sparkling orange

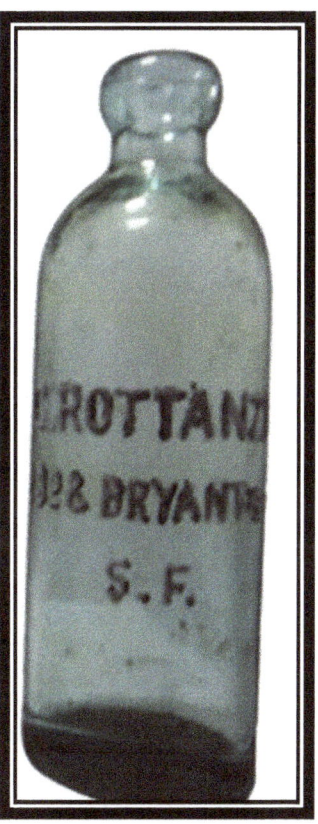

Steve & Christie Curtiss Collection

SAN FRANCISCO
STANDARD SODA WORKS

Face:	STANDARD
	SODA WORKS
	A
	C M
	M
	S. F.
Reverse:	Blank
Bottom:	A
	C M
	M

All letters inside Maltese Cross

Color:	Aqua
Circa:	1890 – 1906
Locality:	San Francisco
Rarity:	Common
Value:	$_____
Markota:	Page 130

Charles Matthews started Standard Soda Works in 1889 with brother Arthur joining in 1890. Located at 1134-1136 Valencia Street moving a few doors down to 1474-1476 Valencia. The business was devastated by the 1906 Earthquake & Fire never to reopen

Steve & Christie Curtiss Collection

SAN FRANCISCO
ROYAL SODA WATER WORKS

Face: **ROYAL**
SODA WATER WORKS
INC.
S.F. CAL.
THIS BOTTLE
NOT TO BE SOLD

Reverse: Blank
Bottom: Blank
Color: Aqua
Circa: 1903
Location: San Francisco
Rarity: Extremely Rare
Value: $_____
Markota: Unlisted

DISAPPOINTED IN BUSINESS VENTURES HE FIRES A REVOLVER BULLET INTO HIS BRAIN

Disappointed in the outcome of a business venture, Louis Leichsenring, a shoemaker, committed suicide yesterday morning by shooting himself through the head with a revolver.

His wife said to Deputy Coroner Michael Brown that Leichsenring three weeks ago invested $1000 for a half interest in the **Royal Soda** Works, owned by Henry Young, at 75 Valley Street, but since removed to 214 Fourteenth street.

The venture proved unprofitable and Leichsenring became despondent. Between 9 and 10 o'clock yesterday morning he went into the basement of his residence, 256 Richland Avenue, and shot himself through the right temple.

He leaves a wife and three children. He was 50 years of age and a native of Germany.

Steve & Christie Curtiss Collection

SAN FRANCISCO
SAN FRANCISCO SODA WORKS

Face:	SAN FRANCISCO SODA WORKS
Reverse:	Blank
Bottom:	S & F
Color:	Aqua & Light green
Circa:	1868 – 1908
Locality:	San Francisco
Rarity:	Common
Value:	Aqua $_____
Value:	Light green $_____
Markota:	Page 117

Started in 1868 by Benjamin Ellerkamp, Nickolos Gierdes & Andrew Ditz at 22 Hinckley Street. In 1873 John N. Gerdes was owner until 1877 having moved to 733 Union Street. In 1878 Henry Gerdes, John's son, and William Bruning were partners until William left in 1879. Bruning moved the company to 323 Francisco Street and took on Henry Schaller as partner.

Bruning died after the signing and his wife Annie became a partner. Schaller sold in 1889 to Frederick Witthack and this partnership lasted until 1892 when Schaller left and Henry Miesner became a partner with Witthack until 1897 and the company had moved to 433 Francisco Street. In 1889 Miesner left the company and Witthack sold to Charles & Henry Stelling and the building was destroyed in 1906 by fire.

Barthold Stelling, one of the sons, tried to reopen in 1907 after the fire & earthquake and reopened at 313 Broderick Street until 1908.

John Burton Collection

Steve & Christie Curtiss Collection

SAN JOSE

SAN JOSE SODA WORKS

Face:	SAN JOSE SODA WORKS
	JOHN BALZHAUSER
	PROP.
	SAN JOSE, CAL.
Reverse:	Blank
Bottom:	J. B.
Color:	Aqua
Circa:	1870's – 1911
Locality:	San Jose, Cal
Rarity:	Scarce
Value:	$_____
Markota:	Page 118

The San Jose Soda Works was established by George Stenger in the late 1870's operating it until 1878. Benthaser Hegle Jr. owned it in 1878 until 1893 located at 356 Marliere Street.

John Balzhauser purchased the soda works and moved it to 344 Provost Street in 1893 selling various carbonated drinks until 1906 selling to August J. Henry who moved to 133 Locust Street until 1911.

Steve & Christie Curtiss Collection

SAN JOSE

C. F. RILEY & CO. BOTTLING WORKS

Face:	C. F. RILEY
	EAGLE
	SODA WORKS
Reverse:	Blank
Bottom:	Blank
Color:	Aqua
Circa:	1890's
Locality:	San Jose, Eureka and San Bernadino
Rarity:	Scarce
Value:	$_____
Markota:	Pages 111 - 112

Charles Riley & at times brother Louis were in Eureka, San Bernadino & San Jose California. They also had a bottling plant in Arizona at one time also.

Left - Eddie Kuskie Collection
Right – Steve & Christie Curtiss Collection

SAN JOSE

WILLIAMS BROS.
(BOTTLE ON LEFT)

Face	WILLIAMS BROS. SAN JOSE CAL.
Reverse:	Blank

Left Bottle Bottom:
GRAVITATING STOPPER MADE BY JOHN MATTHEWS PAT. OCT. 11, 1864 NEW YORK

Color:	Aqua & Light Green
Circa:	1871 – 1910
Locality:	San Jose, Cal.

Left Side Rarity: Common

Value:	$_____
Markota:	Page 144

(BOTTLE ON RIGHT)

Face	WILLIAMS BROS. SAN JOSE CAL.
Reverse:	Blank

Right Bottle Bottom Blank:
Bottle has gravitating body with hutch top
Most likely a "cross-over" bottle
Right side Rarity: Very Rare possibly unique

Value:	$_____

Steve & Christie Curtiss Collection

SAN JOSE

CALIFORNIA SODA WORKS

Face:	CALIFORNIA SODA WORKS SAN JOSE, CAL.
Reverse:	Blank
Bottom:	Large C. S. W.

Comes with & without large slug plate

Color:	Aqua
Circa:	1890 – 1893
Locality:	San Jose, Cal.
Rarity:	Rare
Value:	$_____
Markota:	Page 24

Paul Jeenicke is listed as owner of California Soda Works, San Jose.

Steve & Christie Curtiss Collection

SAN JOSE

	CALIFORNIA SODA WORKS
Face:	PAUL JEENICKE
	SAN JOSE
Reverse:	Blank
Bottom:	P. J.
Color:	Aqua & Amber
Circa:	1890 – 1893
Locality:	San Jose, Cal.
Rarity:	Aqua Rare
	Amber Extremely Rare
Value:	Aqua $_____
	Amber $_____
Markota:	Page 68

Paul Jeenicke was listed at California Soda Works located at northeast corner of Orchard & San Fernando Streets in 1890. In 1893 he was a traveling sales person for Paul Mason selling wholesale liquor & wine. In 1894 he's listed as owner of a boarding house. In 1895 to 1902 he had a saloon and moved to San Francisco in 1902.

Steve & Christie Curtiss Collection

SAN JOSE

	CALIFORNIA SODA WORKS
Face:	CALIFORNIA
	SODA WORKS
	SAN JOSE
	CAL.
Reverse:	Blank
Bottom:	Large C. S. W.
	Comes with & without large slug plate
Color:	Aqua
Circa:	1890 – 1893
Locality:	San Jose, Cal.
Rarity:	Rare
Value:	$_____
Markota:	Page 24

Paul Jeenicke is listed as owner of California Soda Works, San Jose.

Steve & Christie Curtiss Collection

SAN JOSE

GOLDEN WEST SODA WORKS

Face:	GOLDEN WEST SODA WORKS SAN JOSE CAL.
Reverse:	REGISTERED on base
Bottom:	Blank
Base:	THE THOMAS PATENTED DEC. 10-1895
Color:	Light Aqua & Clear
Circa:	1893 – 1920
Locality:	San Jose, Cal.
Rarity:	Rare
Value:	$_____
Markota:	Page 52

Max Schmidt & Theis started Golden West Soda Works in 1893 at 217 Locust Street. Theis left in 1894 and William H. Eberling joined Schmidt in 1900 now located at 209-217 Locust Street. They bottled ginger ale & mineral water, and were agents for Madrone & Aetna Springs.

Steve & Christie Curtiss Collection

SAN LUIS OBISPO

O. TULLMANN'S MINERAL WATER

Face:	O. TULLERMANN'S MINERAL WATER WORKS S. L. O.
Reverse:	Blank
Bottom:	O. T. in monogram
Color:	Aqua, Clear & Sun color
Circa:	1890 – 1920
Locality:	San Luis Obispo, Cal.
Rarity:	Scarce
Value:	$_____
Markota:	Page 138.

Otto O'Tullmann, former saloon owner, started the San Luis Crown Soda Works at 1023 Nipomo Street around 1890. He bottled soda, beer as well as a saloon owner.

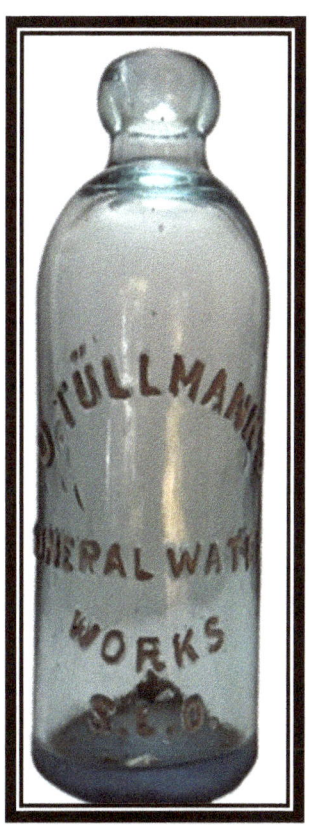

Steve & Christie Curtiss Collection

SAN LUIS OBISPO
CERIBELLI SODA WORKS

Face:	S.L.O.
	SODA WATER
	S. CERIBELLI
Reverse:	Blank
Bottom:	GRAVITATING STOPPER MADE BY JOHN MATTHEWS PAT. OCT. 11, 1864 NEW YORK
Color:	Aqua & Light Green
Circa:	1874 - 1882
Locality:	San Luis Obispo, Cal.
Rarity:	Scarce
Value:	$_____ Aqua
	$_____ Light Green
Markota:	Page 127

Ceribelli was proprietor of San Luis Obispo Soda Work from 1874 to 1882 located on Montgomery Street. He also was a dealer in wine, liquor, tobacco including cigars.

Steve & Christie Curtiss Collection

SAN LUIS OBISPO
SAN LUIS OBISPO SODA WORKS

Face:	S. L. O.
	SODA WORKS
	A. ALBERT
Reverse:	L. G. Co
Bottom:	Blank
Color:	Aqua
Circa:	1883 – 1920
Locality:	San Luis Obispo
Rarity:	Scarce
Value:	$_____
Markota:	Page 128

L. Martin purchased the San Luis Obispo Soda Works from Ceribelli in 1883 located at 969 Islay Street. Martin sold in 1884 to Leopold Albert who was in the grocery business.

John Burton Collection

SAN LUIS OBISPO
SAN LUIS OBISPO BOTTLING WORKS
Face:	**CREAM SODA** (Paper Label)
Reverse:	Blank
Bottom:	Blank
Color:	Aqua
Circa:	1883 – 1920
Locality:	San Luis Obispo
Rarity:	Scarce
Value	$_____
Markota:	Unlisted

Steve & Christie Curtiss Collection

SAN PEDRO
SAN PEDRO SODA & BOTTLING WORKS
Face:	**SAN PEDRO SODA AND BOTTLING WORKS SAN PEDRO, CAL.**
Reverse:	Blank
Bottom:	Blank
Color:	Aqua
Circa:	1890 – 1896
Locality:	San Pedro, Cal.
Rarity:	Extremely Rare
Value:	$_____
Markota:	Page 119

F. M. Hult was proprietor of the San Pedro Soda & Bottling Works. There was only a population of 600 giving reason to his short time in business.

Left – Steve & Christie Curtiss Collection
Right - Eddie Kuskie Collection

SAN PEDRO
STANDARD BOTTLING WORKS

Face:	STANDARD BOTTLING WORKS
	T
	SAN PEDRO, CAL.
	THIS BOTTLE NOT TO BE SOLD
Reverse:	Blank
Bottom:	Blank
Base:	
Color:	Aqua
Circa:	1905 - 1908
Locality:	San Pedro, Cal.
Rarity:	Rare
Value:	$_____
Markota:	Page 131

Another short time soda bottling company in San Pedro.

Left – Steve & Christie Curtiss Collection
Right - Eddie Kuskie Collection

SAN PEDRO
SAN PEDRO WHOLESALE CO.

Face:	SAN PEDRO WHOLESALE CO.
	SAN PEDRO, CAL.
Reverse:	Blank
Bottom:	K
Color:	Aqua
Circa:	1905 - 1920
Locality:	San Pedro, Cal.
Rarity:	Rare
Value:	$_____
Markota:	Page 119

The San Pedro Wholesale Company located in the Sepulveda Building. The water bottles were probably a part of other wholesale items from this company.

Left – Steve & Christie Curtiss Collection
Right - Eddie Kuskie Collection

SAN RAFAEL
BUFFALO BOTTLING WORKS

Face:	BUFFALO
	BOTTLING
	WORKS
	B. B. W.
	SAN RAFAEL
	CALA.
Reverse:	Blank
Bottom:	X
Color:	Aqua
Circa:	1895 – 1912
Locality:	San Rafael, Cal. Marin County
Rarity:	Rare
Value:	$_____
Markota:	Page 21

Borello Brothers opened the Buffalo Bottling Works around 1895 first located on 4th Street between H & F Streets later moving to First & Hates Streets. Andrew was the manager manufacturing sterilized water, various flavored sodas, syphon water and Mt. Tamalpais Mineral Water. The bottling plant was right over the springs.

John Burton Collection

SAN RAFAEL
BUFFALO BOTTLING WORKS

Face:	B. B. W.
	SAN RAFAEL
Reverse:	Blank
Bottom:	Blank
Color:	Aqua
Circa:	1895 – 1912
Locality:	San Rafael, Cal. Marin County
Rarity:	Scarce
Value:	$_____
Markota:	Page 10

Eventually they were listed at 1119 Fourth Street

John Burton Collection

SAN RAFAEL

MARIN SODA WORKS

Face: M. PETERSEN
MARIN
SODA WORKS
SAN RAFAL
Rafael misspelt

Reverse: Blank
Bottom: M. B. W.
Color: Aqua
Circa: 1886 – 1895
Locality: San Rafael, Marin County
Rarity: Very Rare
Value: $_____
Markota: Page 102

As proprietor of the Marin Soda Works, Martin Petersen manufactured carbonated beverages and an agent for Jackson's Napa Soda, Geysers, and Aetna Springs supplying Marin, Sonoma & Mendocino counties.

Steve & Christie Curtiss Collection

SAN RAFAEL

MARIN SODA WORKS

Face: M. PETERSEN
MARIN
SODA WORKS
SAN RAFAEL

Reverse: Blank
Bottom: M. B. W.
Color: Aqua
Circa: 1886 – 1895
Locality: San Rafael, Marin County
Rarity: Semi Common
Value: $_____
Markota: Page 102

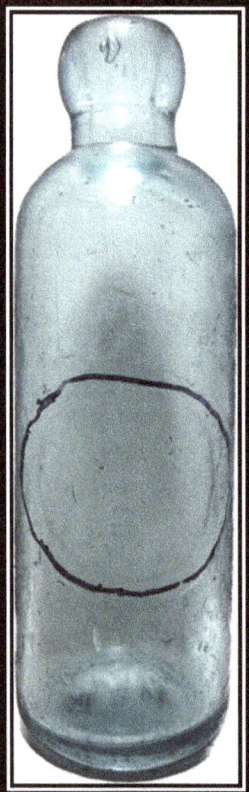

John Burton Collection

SAN RAFAEL

	MARIN SODA WORKS
Face:	M. PETERSEN
	SAN RAFAEL
	CAL.
Reverse:	Blank
Bottom:	M. B. W.
Color:	Aqua
Circa:	1886 – 1895
Locality:	San Rafael, Marin County
Rarity:	Semi Common
Value:	$_____
Markota:	Page 102

John Burton Collection

SAN RAFAEL

	KLAMMER & MALZ
Face:	KLAMMER & MALZ
	SAN RAFAEL,
	CAL.
Reverse:	Blank
Bottom:	M. B. W.
Color:	Aqua
Circa:	1895 – 1905
Locality:	San Rafael, Marin County
Rarity:	Semi Common
Value:	$_____
Markota:	Page 69

Klammer & Malz purchased the Marin Bottling Works from Martin Petersen in 1895 operating it until 1905. The plant was located at 248 D Street and in 1905 Eugene Klammer left going to Petaluma.

John Burton Collection

SANTA ANA

	SANTA ANA SODA WORKS
Face:	GRUMBACH & SCHUMAKER
	SANTA ANA
	CAL.
Reverse:	Blank
Bottom:	Some have X or 329 H
Color:	Aqua
Circa:	1886 - 1887
Locality:	Santa Ana, Cal. Orange County
Rarity:	Extremely Rare
Value:	$_____
Markota:	Page 53

This bottle Schumacher was misspelled.

Isaac M. Grumbach & John Schumacher opened the Santa Ana Soda Works in 1886 at 307 North West Street.

SANTA ANA

	SANTA ANA SODA WORKS
Face:	GRUMBACH & SCHUMACHER
	SANTA ANA
	CAL.
Reverse:	Blank
Bottom:	Some have X or 329 H
Color:	Aqua
Circa:	1886 - 1913
Locality:	Santa Ana, Cal. Orange County
Rarity:	Extremely Rare
Value:	$_____
Markota:	Page 53

This bottle spelled correctly

Grumbach died in 1909 and the soda works was sold to George Wells who had the soda works one year and moved the plant to 1117 West Second Street.

John Schumacher's two sons, John Jr. & Max H. must have repossessed the soda works in 1910 and liquated all remaining assets under the name of Orange County Soda works listed at 308 Sycamore Street

Eddie Kuskie Collection

Eddie Kuskie Collection

SANTA ANA
G. W. WELLS W SANTA ANA

Face: **G. W. WELLS**
W
SANTA ANA

Reverse: Blank
Bottom: Blank
Color: Aqua
Circa: 1901 - 1917
Locality: Santa Ana, Cal. Orange County
Rarity: Very Rare
Value: $_____
Markota: Page 142

Wells started about 1901 on West Third Street. His first product was orange phosphate. About 1910 he purchased the Santa Ana Soda Works from Issac Grumbach & John Schumacher. He then sold in 1917 to Albert Biner.

Steve & Christie Curtiss Collection

SANTA ANA
G. W. WELLS W SANTA ANA

Face: **G. W. WELLS**
W
SANTA ANA

Reverse: Blank
Bottom: 10 Panel mug base
Color: Aqua
Circa: 1901 - 1917
Locality: Santa Ana, Cal. Orange County
Rarity: Very Rare
Value: $_____
Markota: Page 142

Steve & Christie Curtiss Collection

SANTA BARBARA
SANTA BARBARA SODA WORKS

Face:	SANTA BARBARA
	SODA WORKS
	SANTA BARBARA
Reverse:	Blank
Bottom:	Blank
Color:	Aqua
Circa:	1897 – 1920
Locality:	Santa Barbara, Cal.
Rarity:	Extremely Rare
Value:	$_____
Markota:	Page 120

Frank D. Bither established the Santa Barbara Soda Works in 1897 at 512 Garden Street. He manufactured soda water, distilled water, orange phosphate, sarsaparilla, siphon water and Iron water. He was also the sole agent for Celebrated Iron Brew.

Steve & Christie Curtiss Collection

SANTA BARBARA
SANTA BARBARA BOTTLING CO.

Face:	SANTA BARBARA
	BOTTLING Co.
	SANTA BARBARA, CAL.
Reverse:	Blank
Bottom:	33
Color:	Aqua
Circa:	1897 – 1920
Locality:	Santa Barbara, Cal.
Rarity:	Rare
Value:	$_____
Markota:	Page 120

Unable to find the date of the name change from Santa Barbara Soda Works to Santa Barbara Bottling Works.

Steve & Christie Curtiss Collection

SANTA BARBARA
SANTA BARBARA BOTTLING CO.
Face:	SANTA BARBARA BOTTLING Co. SANTA BARBARA, CAL. A. G. W. L.
Reverse:	Blank
Bottom:	33
Color:	Aqua
Circa:	1897 – 1920
Locality:	Santa Barbara, Cal.
Rarity:	Rare
Value:	$_____
Markota:	Page 120

A. G. W. L. is American Glass Works Limited located in Pittsburg, Pennsylvania. Circa 1880 – 1905.

Steve & Christie Curtiss Collection

SANTA BARBARA
CRYSTAL SODA WORKS
Face:	CRYSTAL SODA WORKS (Star with RT) SANTA BARBARA
Reverse:	Blank
Bottom:	Blank
Color:	Aqua
Circa:	1897 – 1920
Locality:	Santa Barbara, Cal.
Rarity:	Rare
Value:	$_____
Markota:	Page 120

Steve & Christie Curtiss Collection

SANTA CRUZ
LODTMANN BROTHERS

Face:	E. & J. LODTMANN SANTA CRUZ Co. CAL.
Reverse:	Blank
Bottom	GRAVITATING STOPPER MADE BY JOHN MATTHEWS PAT. OCT. 11, 1864 NEW YORK
Color:	Aqua
Circa:	1875 – 1890
Locality:	Santa Cruz, Cal.
Rarity:	Scarce
Value:	$_____
Markota:	Page 73

Ernest & Justus Lodtmann were in soda business at Knights Ferry around 1867 to early 1870's. They operated a short time in Modesto moving to Santa Cruz in 1875.

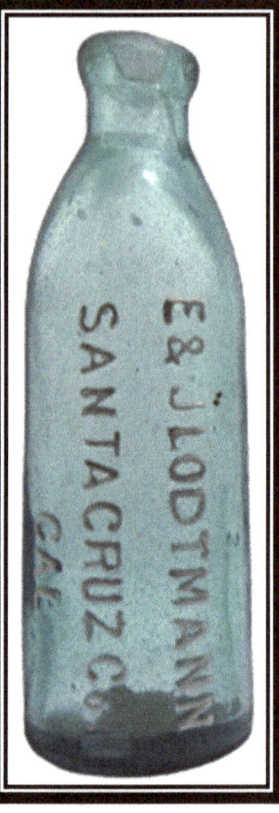

Left – John Burton Collection
Right - Steve & Christie Curtiss Collection

SANTA CRUZ
LODTMANN BROTHERS

Face:	J. LODTMANN SANTA CRUZ Co. CAL.
Reverse:	Blank
Bottom	GRAVITATING STOPPER MADE BY JOHN MATTHEWS PAT. OCT. 11, 1864 NEW YORK
Color:	Aqua
Circa:	1875 – 1890
Locality:	Santa Cruz, Cal.
Rarity:	Scarce
Value:	$_____
Markota:	Page 73

Ernest left around 1885 with Justus operating the soda works until 1890 selling to Peter Wesselhoeft.

Steve & Christie Curtiss Collection

SANTA CRUZ

	LODTMANN BROTHERS
Face:	P. WESSELHOEFT
	SANTA CRUZ Co.
	CAL.
Reverse:	Blank
Bottom	GRAVITATING STOPPER MADE BY JOHN MATTHEWS PAT. OCT. 11, 1864 NEW YORK
Color:	Aqua
Circa:	1875 – 1890
Locality:	Santa Cruz, Cal.
Rarity:	Scarce
Value:	$_____
Markota:	Page 73

SANTA CRUZ

	SANTA CRUZ SODA WORKS
Face:	P. WESSELHOEFT
	SANTA CRUZ Co.
	CAL.
Variant:	WESSELHOEFT
	Slugged into some Lodtmann Bottles
Reverse:	Blank
Bottom:	Some have W and some 6R Lo
Color:	Aqua
Circa:	1890 - 1904
Locality:	Santa Cruz, Cal.
Rarity:	Slug Plate Rare
	No Slug Plate Scarce
Value:	$_____ Slug Plate
	$_____ Non- Slug Plate
Markota:	Page: 143

Peter Wesselhoeft acquired the Santa Cruz Soda Works in 1890 located at 280 Soquel Avenue selling in 1904 to Julius Jacob and went into the saloon business.

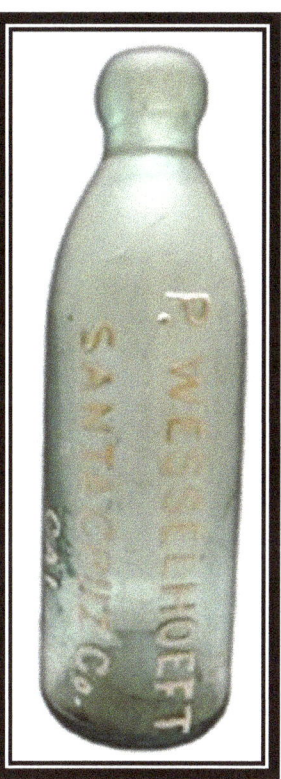 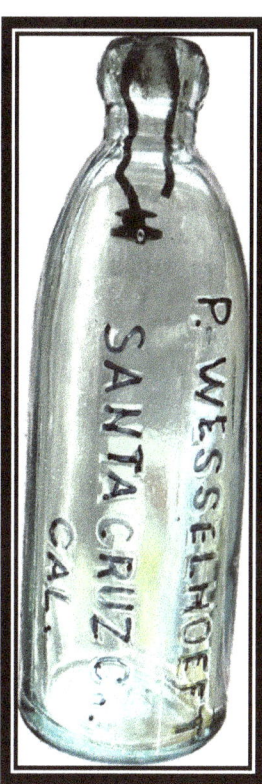

Left Steve & Christie Curtiss Collection
Right Gifted to John Burton by the Curtiss's

Steve & Christie Curtiss Collection

SANTA CRUZ

J. J. SODA WORKS

Face: SANTA CRUZ
J. J.
SODA WORKS
SANTA CRUZ
CAL.

Reverse: Blank
Bottom: P. C. G. W.
Color: Aqua
Circa: 1904 – 1906
Locality: Santa Cruz, Cal.
Rarity: Extremely rare
Value: $_____
Markota: Page 121

When Julius a. Jacob acquired the Santa Cruz Soda Works from Peter Wesselhoeft in 1904, he was out of business in 1906.

A. T. Grove & George Hauselt were the new owners and bottled into the mid-1920's.

Steve & Christie Curtiss Collection

SANTA CRUZ

PACIFIC SODA WORKS

Face: PACIFIC SODA WORKS
R
SANTA CRUZ
Reverse: 33
Bottom: Blank
Color: Aqua
Circa: 1890 -1910
Locality: Santa Cruz, Cal.
Rarity: Semi Rare
Value: $_____
Markota: Page 99

Possibly owned by the National Bottling Works located at 24 Vine Street and R stands for Anton Reiner.

John Burton Collection

SANTA CRUZ
PACIFIC SODA WORKS

Face: PACIFIC SODA WORKS
                             P
                         SANTA CRUZ

Reverse: 33-I G Co. near base.
Bottom: Blank
Color: Aqua
Circa: 1890 -1910
Locality: Santa Cruz, Cal.
Rarity: Semi Rare
Value: $_____
Markota: Page 99

Possibly owned by the National Bottling Works with P standing for Pacific.

33-I. G. Co. means Illinois Glass Company, Alton, Illinois.

John Burton Collection

SANTA CRUZ
EAGLE SODA WATER & BOTTLING CO.

Face: EAGLE
                        Eagle image
                        SODA WATER
                           AND
                        BOTTLING CO.
                       SANTA CRUZ, CAL.

Reverse: Blank
Bottom: Blank
Base: THIS BOTTLE NEVER SOLD
Variant: Without THIS BOTTLE NEVER SOLD
Color: Aqua
Circa: 1906 -1918
Locality: Santa Cruz, Cal.
Rarity: Common
Value: $_____
Markota: Page 37

William E. Atkinson started the Eagle Soda Water & Bottling Works at 19 Cayuga Street in Santa Cruz. He moved to 351 Soquel Street and manufactured various types of soda water until 1918.

John Burton Collection

SANTA CRUZ

EAGLE SODA WATER & BOTTLING CO.

Face:
EAGLE
Eagle image
SODA WATER
AND
BOTTLING CO.
SANTA CRUZ, CAL.

Reverse: Blank
Bottom: Blank
Base: Blank
Color: Aqua
Circa: 1906 -1918
Locality: Santa Cruz, Cal.
Rarity: Common
Value: $_____
Markota: Page 37

Steve & Christie Curtiss Collection

SANTA CRUZ

BITHER BROS.

Face:
BITHER BRO.
SANTA CRUZ
CAL.

Reverse: Blank
Bottom: Blank
Color: Aqua
Circa: 1905 – 1910
Locality: Santa Cruz or Santa Barbara
Rarity: Extremely Rare
Value: $_____
Markota: Page 15

It is believed that the bottles were filled in Santa Barbara and shipped to Santa Cruz. Frank Bither was listed as proprietor and brother William as bottler at the Santa Barbara Soda & Bottling Works.

Steve & Christie Curtiss Collection

SANTA MARIA

SANTA MARIA SODA WORKS

Face:	F. BAUMAN SODA WIORKS SANTA MARIA, CAL.
Reverse:	Blank
Bottom:	B. P.
Variant:	Some have F. B. on bottom
Color:	Aqua
Circa:	1890 – 1912
Locality:	Santa Maria, Cal. Santa Barbara Co.
Rarity:	Rare
Value:	$_____
Markota:	Page 11

Ferdinand Bauman opened the Santa Maria Soda Works at 109 East Chappell Street around 1890. He bottled various sodas, ginger ale and Cordials until 1912.

In 1913 he sold to J. P. Loustalot who operated the business into the mid-1920's.

Steve & Christie Curtiss Collection

SANTA MONICA

SANTA MONICA BOTTLING WORKS

Face:	SANTA MONICA BOTTLING WORKS
Reverse:	Blank
Bottom:	S.M.B.W.
Color:	Aqua
Circa:	1900 - 1908
Locality:	Santa Monica, Cal. Los Angeles Co.
Rarity:	Extremely rare
Value:	$_____
Markota:	Page 121

C. A. Tegner is listed as proprietor of the Santa Monica Soda Works from 1900 until 1908.

Prior to Tegner, Santa Monica Soda Works is listed to C. F. Schafer & Company manufacturing soda as well as selling beers, wine & liquors.

Eddie Kuskie Collection

SANTA ROSA

	T & H SONOMA
Face:	T & H SONOMA CAL.
Reverse:	Blank
Bottom:	GRAVITATING STOPPER MADE BY JOHN MATTHEWS PAT. OCT. 11, 1864 NEW YORK
Color:	Aqua
Circa:	1876 - 1878
Locality:	Santa Rosa, Cal. Sonoma County
Rarity:	Extremely Rare
Value:	$_____
Markota:	Page 134

John Thomas & H. A. Haskins located at 112- 2nd Street. The word "SONOMA" on the face of the bottle was and area guaranteed by John Matthews bottle manufacturer that he would not sell any bottles in Sonoma County other than to Thomas & Haskins.

John Burton Collection

SANTA ROSA

	T & Co. SONOMA
Face:	T & Co. SONOMA CAL.
Reverse:	Blank
Bottom:	GRAVITATING STOPPER MADE BY JOHN MATTHEWS PAT. OCT. 11, 1864 NEW YORK
Color:	Aqua & Teal Blue
Circa:	1878 - 1882
Locality:	Santa Rosa, Cal. Sonoma County
Rarity:	Extremely Rare
Value:	$_____
Markota:	Page 133

Thomas bottled a complete line of soda water, sarsaparilla, bar syrups, ginger ale, and Champagne Cider. Haskins left the company in 1878 and Thomas became the principal owner.

John Burton Collection

SANTA ROSA
P. J. SULLIVAN SONOMA CAL.

Face:	P. J. S. & Co.
	SONOMA
	CAL.
Reverse:	Blank
Bottom:	GRAVITATING STOPPER MADE BY JOHN MATTHEWS PAT. OCT. 11, 1864 NEW YORK
Color:	Aqua & Lime Green
Circa:	1875 – 1882
Locality:	Santa Rosa & Healdsburg County
Rarity:	Very Rare
Value:	$_____
Markota:	Page 104

Located at 160 Third Street between A and B Streets. Patrick J. Sullivan closed his Santa Rosa plant in 1882 going to Healdsburg partnering with brother James Sullivan bottling in September 1883. Believe that this bottle was used in Healdsburg as most have been found there.

John Burton Collection

SANTA ROSA
P. J. SULLIVAN SANTA ROSA, CAL.

Face:	P. J. SULLIVAN
	SANTA ROSA
	CAL.
Reverse:	Blank
Bottom:	GRAVITATING STOPPER MADE BY JOHN MATTHEWS PAT. OCT. 11, 1864 NEW YORK
Color:	Aqua & Lime Green
Circa:	1885 – 1882
Locality:	Santa Rosa, Sonoma County
Rarity:	Rare
Value:	$_____
Markota:	Page 132

John Burton Collection

SANTA ROSA

FORD & JOHNSON SODA WORKS

Face:	Blank
Reverse:	Blank
Bottom:	F. & J. SANTA ROSA
Color:	Aqua
Circa:	1882
Locality:	Santa Rosa, Cal. Sonoma County
Rarity:	Common
Value:	$_____
Markota:	Page 49

George Ford & Conrad Johnson purchased John Thomas's soda works in 1882 staying at 112 Second Street.

In 1883 Ford & Johnson leased the old Placer Brewery and commenced the manufacture of soda, sarsaparilla, ginger ale, bar syrup, etc.

In 1885 Johnson left the company and William Ashley joined Ford until 1887.

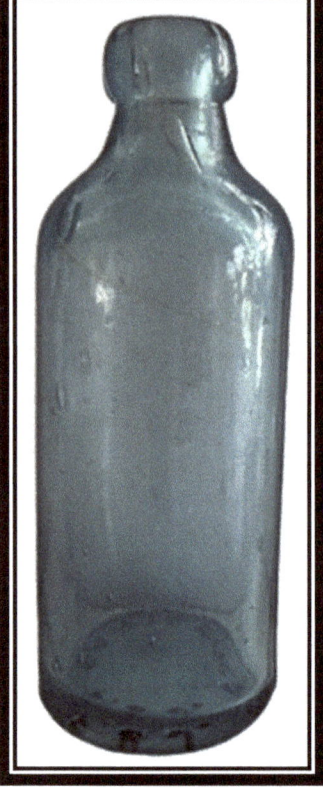

John Burton Collection

SANTA ROSA

HUDSON & PALMER BOTTLING CO.

Face:	HUDSON & PALMER SANTA ROSA BOTTLING CO. SANTA ROSA
Reverse:	33
Bottom:	Blank
Color:	Aqua
Circa:	1887 – 1924
Locality:	Santa Rosa, Cal. Sonoma County
Rarity:	Very Rare
Value:	$_____
Markota:	Page 63

William H. Hudson & his father-in-law were proprietors of the Santa Rosa Bottling Works located at 112 Second Street purchasing the business of Ford & Ashley. They relocated the bottling plant to West Third & Roberts Avenue in 1889.

John Burton Collection

SANTA ROSA

HUDSON & PALMER BOTTLING CO.

Face: HUDSON & PALMER
SANTA
ROSA
BOTTLING CO.
SANTA ROSA

Slightly different style embossing

Reverse:	Blank
Bottom:	Blank
Color:	Aqua
Circa:	1887 – 1924
Locality:	Santa Rosa, Cal. Sonoma County
Rarity:	Very Rare
Value:	$_____
Markota:	Page 63

Hudson had been a hotel keeper in Ukiah moving to Tulare working at the Tulare Bottling plant then moving to Santa Rosa. In Santa Rosa he was in the retail cigar business and a partner in a saloon.

John Burton Collection

SANTA ROSA

SANTA ROSA BOTTLING CO.

Face: SANTA ROSA BOTTLING CO.
Monogram SRBCo.
SANTA ROSA, CAL.
REGISTERED

Reverse:	Blank
Bottom:	Some are plain or 329 H
Color:	Aqua
Circa:	1887 – 1924
Locality:	Santa Rosa, Cal. Sonoma County
Rarity:	Semi Common
Value:	$_____
Markota:	Page 122

After Hudson's father-in-law passed away, the company name was changed to Santa Rosa Bottling Company. As the major bottler in Sonoma County, he bottled various sodas and also bottled oysters.

John Burton Collection

SANTA ROSA
SANTA ROSA BOTTLING CO.

Face:	SANTA ROSA BOTTLING CO.
	Monogram SRBCo.
	SANTA ROSA, CAL.
	Co. in logo appears upside down
Reverse:	Blank
Bottom:	Blank
Color:	Aqua
Circa:	1887 – 1924
Locality:	Santa Rosa, Cal. Sonoma County
Rarity:	Rare
Value:	$_____
Markota:	Page 122

John Burton Collection

SANTA ROSA
SANTA ROSA BOTTLING CO.

Face:	SANTA ROSA BOTTLING CO.
	Monogram SRBCo.
	SANTA ROSA, CAL.
	Co. in logo appears upside down
Reverse:	THIS BOTTLE IS NEVER SOLD
Bottom:	Blank
Color:	Aqua
Circa:	1887 – 1924
Locality:	Santa Rosa, Cal. Sonoma County
Rarity:	Extremely Rare
Value:	$_____
Markota:	Page 122

John Burton Collection

SANTA ROSA

PRIDE OF SANTA ROSA

Face:	Paper Label – Orange Soda
Reverse:	Blank
Bottom:	Blank
Color:	Aqua
Circa:	1910 – 1924
Locality:	Santa Rosa, Cal. Sonoma County
Rarity:	Extremely Rare
Value:	$_____
Markota:	Not Listed

John Burton Collection

SANTA ROSA

I X L SODA WORKS

Face:	I X L SODA WORKS STOLLAR BROS. SANTA ROSA
Reverse:	Blank
Bottom:	Blank
Color;	Aqua
Circa:	1889 – 1891
Location:	Santa Rosa, Cal. Sonoma County
Rarity:	Very Rare
Value:	$_____
Markota:	Page 66

Stollars brothers E. & J. and R. H. started the I.X.L. Soda Works in Santa Rosa in 1891 located on Tupper Street between Petaluma Avenue & E Street.

They had a sales force in San Francisco selling most of their soda in the city.

John Burton Collection

SANTA ROSA

GILT EDGE BOTTLING WORKS
SANTA ROSA
CAL.
BOTTLE NEVER SOLD

Reverse:	Blank
Bottom:	Large +
Color:	Aqua
Circa:	1899 - 1900
Locality:	Santa Rosa, Cal. Sonoma County
Rarity:	Very Rare
Value:	$_____
Markota:	Page 50

Saloon owner George Szameitat bottled Gilt Edge at 500 B Street corner of 5th Street. Gilt Edge bottles were never annealed and most have cracks in them.

John Burton Collection

SAUSALITO

MASON & COMPANY

Face:	MASON & Co.
	SAUSALITO
Reverse:	Blank
Bottom:	M M　M M
Color:	Aqua
Circa:	1900 – 1910
Locality:	Sausalito, Cal. Marin Co.
Rarity:	Extremely Rare
Value:	$_____
Markota:	page 78

John Jr. & Clinton Mason proprietors of Sausalito Soda Works located on Alameda Point. They also owned the Mason Malt Whiskey Distilling Co. managed by John Jr.

1911 out of the soda business but now owners of the Mason Distillery Company located at Alamo & Bolinas Streets.

Composite

SELMA

SELMA SODA WORKS

Face: MORGAN & Co.
SELMA, CAL.
Reverse: Blank
Bottom: Blank
Color: Aqua
Circa: 1905 - 1920
Locality: Selma, Cal. Fresno County
Rarity: Rare
Value: $_____
Markota: Page 85

Andrew L. Morgan established the Selma Soda Works on the Whitson Block, corner of 2nd Street. He moved to 1957 High Street in 1911.

As proprietor of Morgan & Company he also was involved with Joseph L. Reichard owning the Airdrome Picture Theater at 1960 High Street. The Airdrome Theater lasted one year. Morgan continued the soda business until 1920.

Steve & Christie Curtiss Collection

SISSON

MT. SHASTA SODA WORKS

Face: MT. SHASTA SODA WORKS
SISSON, CAL.
Reverse: Blank
Bottom: +
Color: Aqua
Circa: 1880 - 1890
Locality: Sisson, Cal. Mt. Shasta County
Rarity: Rare
Value: $_____
Markota: Page 86

Charles J. Cullen established the Sisson Soda Works in 1880 struggling for two years. His address is listed in Berryville before the town was known as Mt. Shasta. He sold to Peter Mugler in 1890.

Cullen bottled soda, sarsaparilla, ginger ale, cream soda & birch beer.

Steve & Christie Curtiss Collection

SONOMA
SONOMA VALLEY SODA WORKS

Face: SONOMA VALLEY
SODA WORKS
SONOMA
CAL.

Reverse: Blank
Bottom: Blank
Locality: Sonoma, Cal. Sonoma County
Rarity: Extremely rare
Value: $_____
Markota: Page 129

John W. Kelly was the proprietor of the Sonoma Valley Soda Works as well as the Sonoma Valley Ice & Cold Storage company.

SONOMA
SONOMA VALLEY SODA WORKS

Face: BAY VIEW BOTTLING
WORKS
SEATTLE, WASH.

Reverse: Blank
Bottom: 389H
Acid etched on shoulder: S. V. S. W.
SONOMA
CAL.

Base: Ten-paneled bottle
Locality: Sonoma, Cal. Sonoma County
Rarity: Semi rare
Value: $_____
Markota: Page 133

Bay View Bottling Works in Seattle, Washington went out of business and the bottles were purchased by John Kelley of the Sonoma valley Soda Works and acid etched on the left shoulder.

John Burton Collection

**John Burton Collection on left
Steve & Christie Curtiss Collection right**

179

SONORA

SONORA SODA WORKS

Face:	LEONARD
	SONORA
	CAL.
Reverse:	Blank
Bottom:	L
Color:	Aqua & Lime
Circa:	1870 - 1907
Locality:	Sonora, Cal. Tuolumne Co.
Rarity:	Aqua Common
	Lime Extremely Rare
Value:	$_____ Aqua
Value:	$_____ Lime
Markota:	Page 69

Thomas Leonard purchased the Sonora Soda Works in 1870 from the Merriam Brothers. Located on Washington Street Owen Thomas' son took over operations in 1905. In 1907 Owen sold to Michael Terzich.

SONORA

SONORA SODA WORKS

Face:	THOMAS LEONARD
	SONORA
	SODA WORKS
	SONORA, CAL.
Reverse:	Blank
Bottom:	Blank
Color:	Aqua
Circa:	1870 - 1907
Locality:	Sonora, Cal. Tuolumne Co.
Rarity:	Common
Value:	$_____
Markota:	Page 70

Steve & Christie Curtiss Collection

Steve & Christie Curtiss Collection

SONORA

SONORA SODA WORKS

Face: **THOMAS SODA WORKS**
SONORA
CAL.

Reverse: Blank
Bottom: Blank
Color: Aqua
Circa: 1870 - 1907
Locality: Sonora, Cal. Tuolumne Co.
Rarity: Common
Value: $_____
Markota: Page 70

Steve & Christie Curtiss Collection

SONORA

SONORA SODA WORKS

Face: **M. TERZICH**
SONORA
CAL.

Reverse: Blank
Bottom: P.C.G.W.
Color: Aqua
Circa: 1907 - 1960's
Locality: Sonora, Cal. Tuolumne Co.
Rarity: Extremely Rare
Value: $_____
Markota: Page 135

Michael Terzich purchased the Sonora Soda Works from Owen Leonard operating into the 1960's. He also bottled Coca Cola & Delaware Punch.

Steve & Christie Curtiss Collection

SONORA

	SONORA SODA WORKS
Face:	M. TERZICH SONORA, CAL.
	Letters around the base
Reverse:	Blank
Bottom:	P.C.G.W.
Color:	Aqua
Circa:	1907 - 1960's
Locality:	Sonora, Cal. Tuolumne Co.
Rarity:	Extremely Rare
Value:	$_____
Markota:	Page 135

Michael Terzich purchased the Sonora Soda Works from Owen Leonard operating into the 1960's. I imaging this was his first bottle prior to getting one embossed.

Steve & Christie Curtiss Collection

SONORA

	SAMMONS SODA WORKS
Face:	SAMMONS SODA WORKS
	SONORA
	CAL.
Reverse:	Blank:
Bottom:	Blank
Color:	Aqua
Circa:	1900 – 1908
Locality:	Sonora, Cal. Tuolumne Co.
Rarity:	Rare
Value:	$_____
Markota:	Page 114

John & Henry Sammons started the Sammons Brothers soda works in Jamestown around 1894 with Henry moving to Sonora early 1900. Manufacturing all kinds of soda water until 1908 when he sold to sold to John Bacon.

Steve & Christie Curtiss Collection

SONORA

BACON'S SODA WORKS

Face:	BACON'S SODA WORKS SONORA, CAL.
Variant:	No comma after SONORA
Reverse:	Blank
Bottom:	Blank
Color:	Aqua
Circa:	1908 - 1915
Locality:	Sonora, Cal. Tuolumne Co.
Rarity:	Scarce
Value:	$_____
Markota:	Page 10

John Bacon purchased the soda water business from Henry Sammons continuing to manufacture soda water, ginger ale, & carbonated drinks at least until 1915.

Left – Steve & Christie Curtiss Collection
Right - Eddie Kuskie Collection

St. HELENA

ST. HELENA SODA WORKS

Face:	ST. HELENA SODA WORKS
Reverse:	Blank
Bottom:	Some have T
Color:	Aqua
Circa:	1888 – 1920
Locality:	St. Helena, Cal. Napa County
Rarity:	Very rare
Value:	$_____
Markota:	132

A. J. Rutledge started the St. Helena Soda Works in 1888 selling in 1889 to Adolph Meyers who sold in 1904 to C. L. Priest. Priest sold to C. E. Stevens in 1912

In 1905 St. Helena Bottling & Cold Storage Company was in business and at this time not known if they were associated.

John Burton Collection

St. HELENA

ST. HELENA BOTTLING & COLD STORAGE CO.

Face:	Paper label GINGER ALE
Reverse:	Blank
Bottom:	Blank
Color:	Aqua
Circa:	1910 – 1920
Locality:	St. Helena, Cal. Napa County
Rarity:	Extremely rare
Value:	$_____
Markota:	Not Listed

The St. Helena Bottling & Cold Storage started using paper labels around 1910. They must have also had orange soda, strawberry soda, & cream soda paper labels as well. Extremely graphic and colorful label.

John Burton Collection

STOCKTON

NATIONAL SODA WORKS

Face:	NATIONAL SODA WORKS
	Image of Horseshoe
Reverse:	Blank
Bottom:	Blank
Color:	Aqua, Clear & Sun Color
Circa:	1879 – 1925
Locality:	Stockton, Cal. San Joaquin, Co.
Rarity:	Common
Value:	$_____
Markota:	Page 87

Founded by Charles Barthman on the corner of North & Center Streets moving to 706 East Weber Avenue late 1890's. He sold to Charles Ziemer in 1906 and the Ziemer family sold in 1925 to Onofrio Russo. Russo changed the name to National Bottling Works & again in 1927 to National Beverage Company.

Steve & Christie Curtiss Collection

STOCKTON - MARYSVILLE
B (Belding)

Face:	B
Reverse:	Blank
Bottom:	GRAVITATING STOPPER MADE BY JOHN MATTHEWS PAT. OCT. 11, 1864 NEW YORK
Color:	Aqua
Circa:	1870 – 1910
Locality:	Stockton & Marysville
Rarity:	Common
Value	$_____
Markota:	Page 9

Charles Belding worked for bottlers Lippincott & Vaughn in Stockton from 1852 to 1855. Belding partnered with another former employee of Lippincott & Vaughn purchasing the Murphy's Soda Works. Belden sold his interest a year later in 1856 returning to Stockton purchasing Vaughn's interest in Lippincott & Vaughn in 1857. The firm of Lippincott & Belding lasted until 1870 when Belding bought out Benjamin Lippincott.

Belding & Lippincott had also been partners in another soda works in Marysville from 1863 until 1894 when Belding became to sole owner. In 1895 this soda works was operated by Charles's brother Lyman.

At the same time in 1895 Belden sold part interest in the Stockton plant to Samuel B. Huskins with the company becoming know as Belden & Huskins Soda Works. Those bottles are embossed H & B M'VILLE. Charles Belding died February 17, 1905 and it appears all operations stopped in 1910.

With lines in letter B

No lines in letter B
Both Bottles Steve & Christie Curtiss Collection

STOCKTON - MARYSVILLE

        B (Belding)
Face: B & Co.
Reverse: Blank
Bottom: Blank
Color: Aqua
Circa: 1870 – 1890
Locality: Stockton & Marysville
Rarity: Very Rare
Value $_____
Markota: Unlisted

Belding & Company. Bottle probably used in both Stockton & Marysville.

Steve & Christie Curtiss Collection

STOCKTON

    Acid Etched on Shoulder
  Attributed to Belding & Company
Face: Blank
Reverse: Blank
Bottom: Blank
Color: Aqua
Circa: 1890
Locality: Stockton
Rarity: Rare
Value $_____
Markota: Unlisted

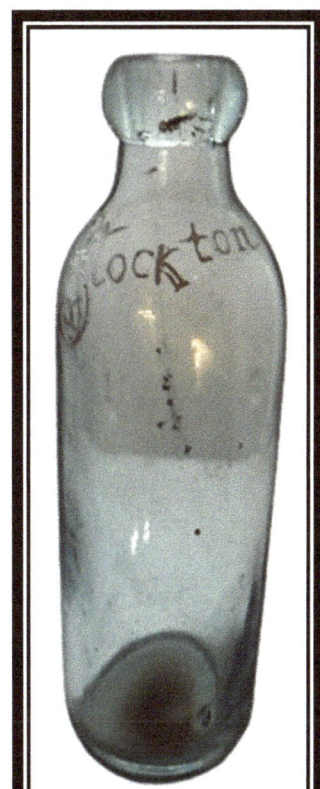

Steve & Christie Curtiss Collection

STOCKTON

B

Face:	B (Belding)
Reverse:	Blank
Bottom:	GRAVITATING STOPPER MADE BY JOHN MATTHEWS PAT. OCT. 11, 1864 NEW YORK
Color:	Aqua
Circa:	1870 – 1910
Locality:	Stockton
Rarity:	Common
Value:	$_____
Markota:	Unlisted

Steve & Christie Curtiss Collection

TRUCKEE

TRUCKEE SODA WORKS

Face:	C. THOMAS TRUCKEE CAL.
Reverse:	Blank:
Bottom:	Blank
Color:	Aqua
Circa:	1885 – 1920
Locality:	Truckee, Cal. Nevada Co.
Rarity:	Rare
Value:	$_____
Markota:	Page 136

Charles Thomas started the Truckee Soda Works & Eureka Brewery around 1885. He manufactured soda, ginger ale, sarsaparilla, and various beers into the 1920's.

Steve & Christie Curtiss Collection

TRUCKEE

	TRUCKEE SODA WORKS
Face:	C. THOMAS
	TRUCKEE
Reverse:	Blank:
Bottom:	Blank
Color:	Aqua
Circa:	1885 – 1920
Locality:	Truckee, Cal. Nevada Co.
Rarity:	Rare
Value:	$_____
Markota:	Page 137

Steve & Christie Curtiss Collection

TULARE

	TULARE SODA WORKS
Face:	TULARE
	SODA WORKS
Reverse:	Blank
Bottom:	Blank
Color:	Aqua
Circa:	1887 - 1892
Locality:	Tulare, Cal. Tulare County
Rarity:	Scarce
Value:	$_____
Markota:	Page 137

R. N. Hough established the Tulare Soda Works on H Street in 1887. Hough also was listed as dealer of ice.

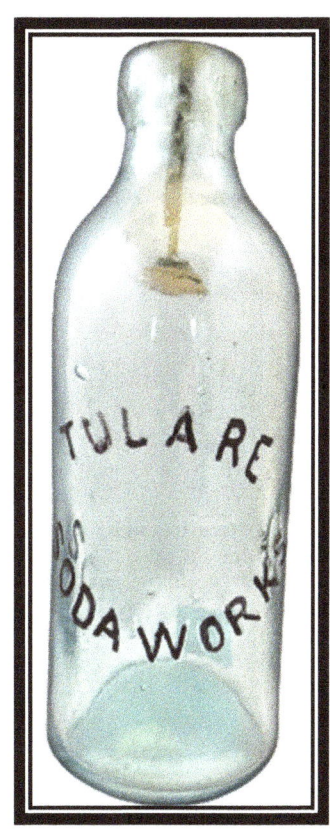

John Burton Collection

UKIAH

	UKIAH SODA WORKS
Face:	UKIAH SODA WORKS UKIAH CAL.
Reverse:	Blank
Bottom:	Blank
Color:	Aqua
Circa:	1874 - 1884
Locality:	Ukiah, Cal. Mendocino Co.
Rarity:	Semi Rare
Value:	$_____
Markota:	Page 138

Sinion Wurtenburg opened & operated the Ukiah City Brewery in 1874 until 1884. There is no information between 1884 to 1907 when Frank & Fritz Ott were proprietors for one year selling to Max Weiss who had been operating the Roseburg Oregon Brewing & Ice Company. Weiss operated the soda works from 1908 into the 1920's.

Large Embossing
John Burton Collection

UKIAH

	UKIAH SODA WORKS
Face:	UKIAH SODA WORKS UKIAH CAL.
Reverse:	Blank
Bottom:	P. C. G. W.
Color:	Light Purple
Circa:	1881 - 1890
Locality:	Ukiah, Cal. Mendocino Co.
Rarity:	Semi Rare
Value:	$_____
Markota:	Page 138

The Ott brothers had been brewers in Island City, Oregon 1889- 1891 and in Enterprise, Oregon 1898 – 1905 prior to becoming involved with the Ukiah Brewing Company. They also had a brother, George Ott who was a brewer in Summerville, Oregon 1896 – 1910. Max Weiss changed the name to Ukiah Brewery & Ice Plant in 1911.

Smaller Embossing
John Burton Collection

UKIAH

GEORGE EPLER SODA WORKS

Face:	G. W. Epler
Reverse:	Blank
Bottom	E
Color:	Aqua
Circa:	1884 – 1890
Locality:	Ukiah, Cal. Mendocino Co.
Rarity:	Semi Rare
Value:	$_____
Markota	Not listed

This bottle seemed to be a travelling universal bottle used in Ukiah, Petaluma, Walla Walla, Salem Oregon & wherever Epler opened a soda business.

John Burton Collection

VACAVILLE

SOLANO SODA WORKS

Face:	SOLANO SODA WORKS VACAVILLE CALIFORNIA
Reverse:	Blank
Bottom:	Blank
Color:	Aqua
Circa:	1903 – 1920
Locality:	Vacaville, Cal. Solano County
Rarity:	Scarce
Value:	$_____
Markota:	Page 128

Started by C. Proctor & L. Larose around 1903 located on Dirker Street. 1910 Larose was the sole proprietor selling to Joseph Manuel in 1911 who operated the business well into the 1920's.

Steve & Christie Curtiss Collection

VALLEJO

	EMPIRE SODA WORKS
Face:	EMPIRE SODA WORKS VALLEJO, CAL.
Reverse:	Blank
Bottom:	Blank
Color:	Aqua
Circa:	1874 - 1890
Locality:	Vallejo, Cal. Solano County
Rarity:	Scarce
Value:	$_____
Markota:	Page 41

Frank & Charles O'Grady established the Empire Soda Works in 1874 corner of Sonoma & Carolina Streets. In 1880 Charles left the business and Frank operated it until 1890. In 1887 the business was relocated to the northeast corner of Sonoma & Florida Streets. F. M. McDermott was a partner for a short time.

John Burton Collection

VALLEJO

	EMPIRE SODA WORKS
Face:	EMPIRE SODA WORKS VALLEJO
Reverse:	Blank
Bottom:	Blank
Color:	Aqua
Circa:	1874 - 1890
Locality:	Vallejo, Cal. Solano County
Rarity:	Scarce
Value:	$_____
Markota:	Page 41

John Burton Collection

VALLEJO

W. TOMEY SODA WORKS

Face: W. TOMEY
VALLEJO
Reverse: Blank
Bottom: Blank
Color: Aqua & Light Green
Circa: 1883 – 1890
Locality: Vallejo, Cal. Solano County
Rarity: Aqua common
Light Green Extremely Rare
Value: $_____ Aqua
$_____ Light Green
Markota: Page 137

William Tormey a former liquor dealer and insurance man began bottling water at the former Pioneer Brewery owned by Edward McGettigan located at corner of Carolina & Marin Streets. He left the business in 1890 purchasing a hotel. The bottling location eventually became home of Empire Soda Works.

John Burton Collection

VENTURA

ACME SODA WORKS VENTURA, CAL.

Face: ACME
SODA WORKS
VENTURA
CAL.
Reverse: Blank
Color: Aqua
Locality: Ventura, Cal.
Circa: 1898 – 1920
Rarity: Extremely Rare
Value: $_____

1898 Floyd P. Shaw purchased the soda works located on the corner of Poi & Hemlock streets. Shaw manufactured Ginger Ale, Sarsaparilla, Iron, Orange Cide and Artificial Mineral water.

In time the company became Shaw & Middlecoff with Shaw as President & Middlecoff Vice President.

Steve & Christie Curtiss Collection

VISALIA

VISALIA SODA WORKS

Face:	VISALIA SODA WORKS
Reverse:	Blank:
Bottom:	Blank
Color:	Aqua
Circa:	1884 – 1920
Locality:	Visalia, Cal. Tulare County
Rarity:	Rare
Value:	$_____
Markota:	Page 139

Thomas J. Beaver & William H. Hudson established the Visalia Soda Works on South Street in 1884 with Hudson leaving soon to purchase the Santa Rosa Bottling Works with his father-in-law James Palmer. Beaver relocated the bottling plant to 417 East South Street operating by himself until he sold to Jessie L. Frame of the Porterville Soda Works now located at Bridge & Oak Street.

Steve & Christie Curtiss Collection

WATSONVILLE

MARTINELLI & COMPANY

Face:	S MARTINELLI WATSONVILLE
Reverse:	Blank
Bottom:	Blank
Color:	Aqua
Circa:	1868 – 1950
Locality:	Watsonville, Cal. Santa Cruz Co.
Rarity:	Common
Value:	$_____
Markota:	Page 78

Stephen Martinelli started in 1868 bottling fermented champagne, hard cider & carbonated drinks in his brother's barn. In 1880 he located the business into the center of Watsonville. In 1956 the Martinelli family sold the franchise which is still in business today.

Steve & Christie Curtiss Collection

WATSONVILLE
WATSONVILLE BOTTLING WORKS

Face: WATSONVILLE
BOTTLING WORKS
H. A. P.
PROPRIETOR
Reverse: Blank
Bottom: Blank
Color: Aqua
Circa: 1904 - 1912
Locality: Watsonville, Cal. Santa Cruz Co.
Rarity: Scarce
Value: $_____
Markota: page 141

Henry R. Peterson an agent for Fredericksburg Beer, started bottling soda water at 148 West 4th Street in 1904 until 1913. Henry died and his wife sold the business and it operated into the 1920's.

John Burton Collection

WATSONVILLE
WATSONVILLE BOTTLING WORKS

Face: WATSONVILLE
BOTTLING WORKS
H. A. R.
PROPRIETOR
H. A. R. a misprint
Reverse: Blank
Bottom: Blank
Color: Aqua
Circa: 1904 - 1912
Locality: Watsonville, Cal. Santa Cruz Co.
Rarity: Extremely Rare
Value: $_____
Markota: page 141

H. A. Petersen bottled the first lager beer bottled from the Santa Cruz Brewing Companies new brewery in 1907.

WILLOWS

WILLOWS SODA & BOTTLING WORKS

Face:	WILLOWS BOTTLING WORKS WILLOWS, CAL.
Reverse:	Blank
Bottom:	X
Color:	Aqua
Circa:	1880 – 1897
Locality:	Willows, Cal. Glenn County
Rarity:	Extremely Rare
Value:	$_____
Markota:	Page 145

Mrs. E. H. Keyes & George Brower started the Willows Bottling Soda & Bottling Works in 1880. Brower left in 1881 Mrs. Keyes is listed as proprietor of Willows Soda Works. She sold the business to Selig Dahlman around 1893 who closed it in 1897.

John Burton Collection

WOODLAND

WOODLAND SODA WORKS

Face:	WOODLAND SODA WORKS
Reverse:	Blank
Bottom:	Blank
Color:	Aqua
Circa:	1882 – 1887
Locality:	Woodland, Cal. Yolo County
Rarity:	Rare:
Value:	$_____
Markota:	Page 146

Listed as the proprietor in 1882 was A. Brown. In 1888 Carey Barney was listed as the new owner.

John Burton Collection

WOODLAND

WOODLAND SODA WORKS

Face: **O. A.**
WOODLAND

Reverse: Blank
Bottom: Blank
Color: Aqua
Circa: 1904 – 1910
Reverse: Blank
Bottom: **GRAVITATING STOPPER MADE BY JOHN MATTHEWS PAT. OCT. 11, 1864 NEW YORK**

Steve & Christie Curtiss Collection

WOODLAND

WOODLAND SODA WORKS

Face: **C. M. B.**
WOODLAND

Reverse: Blank
Bottom: Blank
Color: Aqua
Circa: 1888 – 1890
Locality: Woodland, Cal. Yolo County
Rarity: Rare
Value: $_____
Markota: Page 30

Carey M. Barney, a former Sherriff of Woodland, is listed as the proprietor in 1888 having purchased the business from A. Brown.

In 1890 Barney sold to George Hitchcock who operated the bottling works until 1904 and Barney became City Marshall of Woodland.

Steve & Christie Curtiss Collection

YREKA
BONNAVENTURE GUILBERT SODA FACTORY

Face: B. GUILBERT
   YREKA
Reverse: Blank
Bottom: Blank
Color: Aqua
Circa: 1890 - 1898
Locality: Yreka, Cal. Siskiyou, County
Rarity: Extremely Rare
Value: $_____
Markota: Page 54

Bonnaventure Guilbert bottled soda on Miner Street from approximately 1890 to 1898. He passed away in 1898 and his wife operated the soda factory possibly to the Meamber brothers.

Steve & Christie Curtiss Collection

YREKA
MEAMBER BROTHERS YREKA SODA WORKS

Face: MEAMBER BROS.
   PINEAPPLE SODA
   YREKA, CAL.
Reverse: Blank
Bottom: Blank
Color: Aqua
Circa: 1887 – 1971
Locality: Yreka, Cal. Siskiyou County
Rarity: Extremely Rare
Value: $_____
Markota: Unlisted Paper Label

Bob Voegtly Collection

YREKA
MEAMBER BROTHERS YREKA SODA WORKS

Face:	MEAMBER BROS. YREKA
Reverse:	Blank
Bottom	+
Color:	Aqua
Circa:	1887 – 1971
Locality:	Yreka, Cal. Siskiyou County
Rarity:	Extremely Rare
Value:	$_____
Markota:	Page 80

Fred J. & George B. Meamber founded their Table Rock Spring Water 18 miles from Yreka in 1887. Fred moved to Richmond California around 1910 & purchased the Richmond Bottling Works owning it for only six months.

Fred rejoined the Yreka Soda Works and the brothers operated it until 1924 the business became known as the Coca Cola Bottling Works until 1971.

The brothers also purchased the Mugler Soda Works in Mt. Shasta in 1927 becoming the owners of the Seven-Up franchise until 1932.

Steve & Christie Curtiss Collection

BURTON & CURTISS HUTCH AND GRAVITATING STOPPER INDEX

ALAMEDA — Page 1-3
ALAMEDA/ (Hands shaking) / SODA WATER CO./BOTTLE'S IS NOT SOLD
ALAMEDA/(Hands shaking) / SODA WATER CO./BOTTLE IS NOT SOLD
EMPIRE SODA WORKS/ WEISS & Co.
EMPIRE SODA WORKS/ ALAMEDA/ CAL.
EMPIRE SODA WORKS/ ALAMEDA

ALTURAS — Page 3
ALTURAS/ SODA WORKS/ ALTURAS/ CAL.

AMADOR — Page 4
AMADOR COUNTY/ SODA WORKS

ANGEL'S CAMP — Page 4-5
ANGEL'S BREWERY/ AND/ SODA WORKS/E.F. HUBLER/ PROP.
SEQUOIA/ SODA WORKS/ ANGELS/ CAL.

ANTIOCH — Page 5
PIONEER/ SODA WORKS/ ANTIOCH

ARCATA — Page 6
ARCATA/ B.P. /SODA WORKS

AUBURN — Page 6-7
J. & R./ AUBURN (On bottom)
A. W. K. & CO./ AUBURN/ CAL. (On bottom)

BAKERSFIELD — Page 7
H. F. CONDICT/ BAKERSFIELD

BAKERSFIELD – SUMNER — Page 8
G. GALLI/ SODA WORKS /SUMNER/ &/ BAKERSFIELD

BELMONT — Page 8
BELMONT/ SODA WORKS/ TRADE (Horseshoe) MARK /CAL.

BENICIA — Page 9
BENICIA /STEAM /SODA WORKS/GUSTAV GNAUCK

BERKELEY — Page 9-11
R. L. AGERS/ & Co./ A. C. (Monogram)/ BERKELEY CAL.
GILBERT HALL /BERKELEY /CAL.
BERKELEY SODA /WORKS/ A & K/ BERKELEY/ CAL
ARTIC /SODA WATER Co./ BERKELEY /CAL.

BLACK DIAMOND — Page 11
BLACK DIAMOND/ ^I /SODA WORKS

BISHOP — Page 12
T. SHONE
INYO SODA WORKS /BISHOP CAL.

BODIE — Page 13
PEARSON BROS. /BODIE

CHICO — Page 13-14
A. F. BLOOD/ CHICO, CAL.

CHICO SODA /WORKS

COLUSA — Page 14-15

COLUSA SODA /WORKS /COLUSA, /CAL.
J. W. DAVIS/ COLUSA, CAL.

CROCKETT — Page 15

CROCKETT /(Star Monogram) /SODA WORKS

DIXON — Page 16

DIXON/ SODA WORKS

EL DORADO — Page 16

ELDORADO /BOTTLING CO.

EEL RIVER VALLEY (Springville) — Page 17

EEL RIVER VALLEY /SPRINGVILLE/ CAL./SODA WORKS
EEL RIVER VALLEY/SODA WORKS/SPRINGVILLE, CAL.

EUREKA — Page 18-26

J. P. MONROE & Co. /EUREKA/HUMBOLDT Co./ CAL.
A. MONROE & Co. /EUREKA, H. C./ CAL.
H & M /EUREKA/ CAL.
HUMBOLDT /ARTESIAN /MINERAL WATER/EUREKA, CAL.
MONROE /*CIDER & VINEGAR Co*/. EUREKA, /CAL.
MONROES'/ DISTILLED /SODA WATER/EUREKA, CAL.
CITY/ EUREKA /SODA WORKS
JOHN O'DEA/ EUREKA, CAL/ BOTTLING WORKS
DELANEY & YOUNG/ EUREKA, CAL.
DELANEY & YOUNG (Facsimile)
C. F. RILEY (Cobalt)
C. F. RILEY
C. F. RILEY & Co./ (Eagle) /SODA WORKS
C. F. RILEY /(Eagle) /SODA WORKS
C. F. RILEY / (Different Eagle) /SODA WORKS
BOTTLE NEVER SOLD R MUST BE RETURNED (On bottom)
HUMBOLDT (Testimonial Paper label)

FERNDALE — Page 27

MONROE CIDER /& VINEGAR Co. /FERNDALE/ CAL.

FORTUNA

MONROE BOTTLING /WORKS /FORTUNA, CAL.

FORT BRAGG — Page 28

STANDARD /BOTTLING Co./ FORT BRAGG

FRESNO — Page 29-31

RICHTER'S /BOTTLING WORKS /FRESNO, CAL.
RICHTER'S /BOTTLING/ WORKS /FRESNO, /CALA.
MORIMOTO SODA WORKS /(Japanese script) /FRESNO, CAL.
CALIFORNIA SODA /WORKS/ FRESNO, CAL.
SAN JOAQUIN SODA WATER WORKS/SJSW/FRESNO/CAL.

FULLERTON — Page 32
G. B. HUGGANS /FULLERTON, C/AL.
GILROY
T. HILDEBRAND /GILROY CAL.
GRASS VALLEY — Page 33-34
W. E. DEAMER/ GRASS VALLEY/ CAL. /
W.E. DEAMER
(Reverse) NEVADA /SODA WATER Co./GRASS VLLEY NEVADA Co. /CAL.
R. H. WILLIAMS/ GRASS VALLEY
HANSSEN BROS./G. W. B. /GRASS VALLEY, CAL.
GRIDLEY — Page 35
GRIDLEY /CAL. /SODA WORKS
GRIDLEY /SODA WORKS
HALF MOON BAY — Page 36
Unconfirmed
HANFORD — Page 37
HANFORD /SODA WORKS/ J. S
HANFORD ICE CO. /HANFORD /CAL.
HAYWARD — Page 38
HAYWARDS /J. A. COLLINS /SODA WORKS
HAYWARDS /S. J. SIMMONS/ SODA WORKS
HEALDSBURG — Page 39
F. B./HEALDSBURG /CAL.
F. B. /HEALDSBURG
HOLLISTER — Page 40
HOLLISTER /J. DORN /SODA WORKS
J. DORN /SODA WORKS
JACKSON — Page 41
JACKSON BOTTLING /P & G /WORKS
JAMESTOWN — Page 41
SAMMONS BROS./ JAMESTOWN
KESWICK — Page 42
FINK & MUGLER /BOTTLERS /KESWICK, CAL.
KING CITY — Page 42
P. E. WEAVER/ KING CITY /SODA WORKS
LIVERMORE — Page 43-46
LIVERMORE /SODA/ WORKS
LIVERMORE SODA WORKS /LIVERMORE /CALA.
LIVERMORE SODA WORKS /LIVERMORE /CAL.
LIVERMORE SODA WORKS /(Lamb) /LIVERMORE /CAL.
LODI — Page 46
LODI /SODA WORKS
LOS ANGELES — Page 47-62
LOS ANGELES /(Star) /SODA WORKS (Rolled R)

LOS ANGELES /TRADE (Star) Mark /SODA WORKS/THIS BOTTLE IS REGISTERED NOT TO BE SOLD
LOS ANGELES /(Star) /SODA WORKS (Squatty slug plate)
LOS ANGELES /TRADE (Star) Mark /SODA WORKS
LOS ANGELES /TRADE (Star) MARK/SODA WORKS (Applied top)
CALIFORNIA /S. C. & Co. /SODA WORKS
SODA /S.C. & Co. /SODA WORKS /LOS ANGELES
PACIFIC/ (Anchor facing left)/ SODA WORKS/ L. A. CAL.
PACIFIC / (Anchor tilted left) /SODA WORKS /L. A. CAL. (10-Sided panel)
PACIFIC / (Anchor tilted right) /SODA WORKS /L. A. CAL.
PACIFIC / (Anchor tilting left) /L. A. CAL./BOTTLING WORKS
EXCELSIOR/ SODA WORKS /LOS /ANGELES, CAL. (Large embossing)
EXCELSIOR /SODA WORKS /LOS /ANGELES, CAL. (With & without slug plate)
JAMES /SODA WORKS /LOS ANGELES /CAL.
JAMES /SODA WORKS /LOS ANGELES /CAL.
F. A. HEIM /LOS ANGELES CAL. /BOTTLING WORKS
F. A. HEIM'S/ BOTTLING WORKS
HEIM'S
RAMONA /BOTTLING /WORKS/ LOS ANGELES, CAL.
PURITA'S
SANITAS/ BOTTLING WORKS /LOS ANGELES
LIGHTER'S BOTTLING WORKS /LOS ANGELES, CAL.
CASCADE BOT. WKS. /PEVERLY /BROS. PROP. / LOS ANGLES (Angeles MISSPELT)
NEW YORK/ BOTTLING CO./ J. SCHWARTZ, PROP. /LOS ANGELES, CAL
NEW YORK /BOTTLING WORKS /LOS ANGELES/CAL. THIS BOTTLE NOT TO BE SOLD
NEW YORK /BOTTLING WORKS /LOS ANGELES
CRYSTAL BOTTLING CO. /LOS ANGELES CA.
HYGEIA /MINERAL WATER/ CO. /LOS ANGELES/ CAL.

MADERA   **Page 62-63**
BORELLO & PORTER/ MADERA
MEDERA
BORELLO & PORTER /MEDERA
MARYSVILLE   **Page 63-66**
CHARLES BELDING /B /MARYSVILLE /SODA WORKS
MARYSVILLE /SODA /WORKS
B
H & B
MARTINEZ   **Page 66-67**
XLCR/ SODA (Sheild with star) WORKS
XLCR /SODA (Sheild with star) WORKS /MARTINEZ
MAYFIELD (Palo Alto)   **Page 67**
MAYFIELD /SODA WORKS
MELROSE   **Page 68**
MELROSE /BOTTLING WORKS /J. PRIMUS

MENDOCINO — Page 68-69
MENDOCINO /BOTTLING WORKS /A. L. REYNOLDS
OCEAN VIEW /BOTTLING WORKS /N & B PROPS. / MENDOCINO, CAL.

MILLS — Page 69
MILL'S /SELTZER /SPRINGS

MODESTO — Page 70
STANISLAUS /SODA WORKS /MODESTO, CAL.

MOKELUMNE HILL — Page 70-71
C. A. WERLE /MOK. HILL
MOKELUMNE HILL /SODA WORKS

MOUNTAIN VIEW — Page 71
GOLDEN WEST/SODAWORKS/BRUNS & NASH/ MOUNTAIN VIEW/ CAL.

MONTEREY — Page 72-73
PROPERTY OF /MONTEREY /SODA WORKS /CAL.
MONTEREY /SODA WORKS /CAL.
ENTERPRISE /SODA WATER CO. /MONTEREY

NAPA — Page 74-75
ED HENRY /EH /NAPA, CAL.
A LUDWIG /NAPA /CAL.
A. LUDWIG/ NAPA
WALTER'S /NAPA /COUNTY/ SODA /HUTCHINS /&/ REYNOLDS

NEVADA CITY — Page 76-77
STAR SODA WORKS /(Star) /GRIBBLE & Co. /NEVADA CITY
NEVADA CITY /SODA WORKS /E. T. R. POWELL (Vertical)
NEVADA CITY SODA WORKS/ (Flower) /E. T. R. POWELL
(Reverse) NEVADA CITY SODA WORKS E. T. R. POWELL (Vertical)
NEVADA CITY /ROOT BEER Paper Label

OAKLAND — Page 78-83
J. I. BLEVENS & Co. /OAKLAND CAL.
JOHN D. TAYLOR & Co. /PIONEER SODA /WATER WORKS /OAKLAND /CAL.
TAYLOR & LOHSE /SUCCESORS TO /J. I. BLIVENS & Co. /OAKLAND /CAL.
OAKLAND PIONEER/ CO./ SODA WATER
THE DISTILLED SODA WATER Co. /FIFTH & /KIRKHAM STs /OAKLAND
O. P. S. W. Co./ (Bottle) /REGISTERED /BOTTLE IS NEVER SOLD
OAKLAND PIONEER /(Bottle) S/ODA WATER Co./ BOTTLE IS NEVER SOLD
OAKLAND /LM/ SODA WORKS
OAKLAND /(Sun) /STEAM SODA WORKS /BOTTLE IS NOT TO BE SOLD
SILVER STILL /PURE WATER CO. /OAKLAND

OROVILLE — Page 84
E. HIGGINS /OROVILLE (On bottom)

OCCIDENTAL — Page 84
OCCIDENTAL BOTTLING WORKS /(Monogram)/ OCCIDENTAL, CAL.

ONTARIO — Page 85
O. K./ SODA /WORKS

OXNARD — Page 85
WOOD & BELL / OXNARD, CAL.

PASADENA — Page 86
THE IMPROVED /SODA WORKS/ PASADENA

PASA ROBLES — Page 86
PASA ROBLES SODA WORKS
PASA ROBLES SODA WORKS /PASA ROBLES

PETALUMA — Page 87-89
ENDRES & CO. /PETALUMA, CAL.
CAPITAL SODA /& /BOTTLING /WORKS /PETALUMA /CAL.
CAPITAL BOTTLING WORKS /L. S./ PETALUMA, CAL.
PETALUMA SODA AND SELTZER WORKS/ GINGER ALE (Paper Label)
G. W. EPLER

PLACERVILLE — Page 89-90
PEARSON'S /SODA WORKS (Small print arched)
PEARSON'S/ SODA WORKS (Large print straight)
PEARSON BROS. /PLACERVILLE
PEARSON BROS. / P on reverse

PLYMOUTH — Page 91
PLYMOUTH/ CAL. /SODA WORKS
CHAMPION /SODA WORKS /PLYMOUTH, CAL.

POMONA — Page 92
POMONA /SODA WORKS /POMONA, CAL.
POMONA /SODA WORKS /POMONA, CAL.

POINT RICHMOND — Page 93
RICHMOND SODA WORKS /R. S. W. /POINT RICHMOND

PORT COSTA — Page 93
J. C. /PORT COSTA /SODA WORKS

REDDING — Page 94-95
A. & K. /REDDING (On bottom)
ZEIS & SONS /REDDING, CAL./BOTTLE IS NEVER SOLD
ZEIS & SONS/ REDDING, CAL.

RED BLUFF — Page 95-96
CIRCLE PAULSON & Co. /RED BLUFF /CALA.
D. S. CONE /I & R CO. /R. B.

RIVERSIDE — Page 96
RIVERSIDE /SODA WORKS

SACRAMENTO — Page 97-106
H /P (Reverse blank)
H SAC (Reverse P)
H /SAC. / P
HOLDEN'S /G. A.
UNION SODA WORKS (Paper label) U.S.W./SAC. On bottom

HENRY POSTEL /SACRAMENTO /CAL.
POSTEL & SCHNEER /SACRAMENTO /CAL.
C. SCHNEER & Co. /SACRAMENTO /CAL.
C. SCHNERR & Co./ SACRAMENTO CAL. (Reverse NEVADA CITY SODA WORKS (Flower)E. T. R. POWELL)
E. L. BILLINGS /SACRAMENTO /CAL
OWEN CASEY/ EAGLE SODA/ WORKS (Reverse SAC. CITY)
CASEY & CRONAN /EAGLE /SODA WORKS
HUGH CASEY /(Eagle) /SODA WORKS
HUGH CASEY /(Eagle)/ SODA WORKS/ 50 K ST. /SACRAMENTO /CAL.
CASEY & KAVANUGH /TRADE /MARK /REGISTERED /SACRAMENTO CAL.
M. CRONAN /230 K STREET/ SACRAMENTO
S.C.O.H.N.M.W.ASSN. /TRADE /MARK /REGISTERED/ SACRAMENTO, CAL.
S.C.O.H.N.M.W.ASSN. /SACRAMENTO, CAL.
CALIFORNIA/ BOTTLING WORKS/T. BLAUTH/ 407 K STREET/SACRAMENTO
CALIFORNIA/ BOTTLING WORKS /THEO. BLAUTH & SONS CO./ 407 K STREET/ SACRAMENTO
BERNARD McGINITY/ SACRAMENTO /CAL.
THE GEO. Z. WAIT/ CARBONATING/ CO./ SACRAMENTO, CAL.

SALINAS   Page 107
STEIGELMAN/ P.S./ SALINAS SODA WORKS
SALINAS/ P.S./ SODA WORKS

SAN ANSELMO   Page 108
SAN ANSELMO/ BOTTLING CO./SAN ANSELMO, CAL.
SAN ANSELMO / BOTTLING CO./ SAN RAFAEL, CAL.

SAN BERNARDINO   Page 109-111
BOWLAND & CRAIG/ CITY PHARMACY/ SODA WORKS/ SAN BERNARDINO/ CAL.
AUG. WINKLER/ S. B./ SODA WORKS
C. F. RILEY/ Eagle/ SODA WORKS

SAN DIEGO   Page 112-118
XLCR/ SODA WORKS
F. J. A. SCHMID/ SAN DIEGO/ CAL./ XLCR
P. D. ASHTON/ SAN DIEGO/ CAL./ XLCR
EXCELSIOR BOTTLING/ AND/ EXTRACT CO./ SAN DIEGO/ CAL.
SAN DIEGO SODA WORKS/ TRADE (Star) MARK/ G. GAEDKE & A. SEIFKE
SAN DIEGO SODA WORKS/ TRADE (Star) MARK
SAN DIEGO/ TRADE (Star) MARK/ SODA WORKS (Base G.G.)
SAN DIEGO/ TRADE (Star) MARK/ SODA WORKS (Base S. B. & G. CO.)
SAN DIEGO/ TRADE (Star) MARK/ SODA WORKS (Page 116 #2)
SAN DIEGO/ TRADE (Star) MARK/ SODA WORKS (Page 116 #3)
SAN DIEGO/ TRADE (Star) MARK/ SODA WORKS (Base P. C. G. W.)
BRADLEY/ SPRING WATER/ Eagle/ SAN DIEGO CAL.
BRADLEY/ SPRING WATER Co./ Eagle/ SAN DIEGO, CAL.????

SAN FRANCISCO

AMERICAN/ Flag/ SODA WORKS/S.F.
ASTORG/ SPRINGS/ MINERAL/ WATER/ S. F. – CAL.
BAY CITY SODA WATER Co./ SAN FRANCISCO/ CAL.
BAY CITY SODA WATER Co./ SAN FRANCISCO
THE BELFAST/ SODA WATER &/ GINGER ALE Co./SAN FRANCISCO/ CAL.
BELFAST SODA /TRADE B MARK/ GINGER ALE/ S.F.
(Fish looking right) BREIG & BAUER/ S. F.
BREIG & SCHAFER (Fish looking left) S.F.
CAL. LEMONADE/ C L inside star/AND/ SELTZER WATER CO./S.F. CAL.
CALIFORNIA /(Eagle) /SODA WORKS
CRYSTAL/ SODA/ WATER CO.
CRYSTAL/ S. W. CO./ S. F.
CRYSTAL/ SODA/ WATERR Co. (reverse PATENTED/ NOV. 12, 1872/ TAYLOR'S/ US PI
DIAMOND / TRADE <D> MARK/ SODA WORKS CO./ S.F.
EASTERN/ CIDER Co.
EMPIRE SODA WORKS/ SAN FRANCISCO/ WALDO & CO. (Reverse FRANK/ S/ WALDO & CO.)
ENTERPRISE / SODA WORKS/ S. F. / A. & W. G.
ENTERPRISE / SODA WORKS/ S. F.
ENTERPRISE/ SODA WORKS / S. F. (Reverse K. & G. Co.)
EUREKA / SODA WORKS/ S. F. (Bottom H & H, H)
EUREKA/ SODA WORKS/ S. F. (Bottom Trade (car) Mark)
EUREKA – CALIFORNIA/ Eagle/ SODA WATER CO./ S. F.
EUREKA/ SODA WORKS/ 723 TURK ST. / S.F.
FAIRMONT / SODA WORKS/ S. F.
GARCIA BROS./ S. F./ (Reverse PINE – APPLE/ NECTAR
GLOBE/ MINERAL WATERS/ (Globe image)/ 510 CONNECTICUT ST. S. F./ BOTTLE NOT TO BE SOLD
HERVE & SOMPS/ SAN FRANCISCO/ CAL.
HERVE & SOMPS/ SAN/ FRANCISCO, CAL.
P. SOMPS/ SODA WATER/ WORKS/ S. F. CAL.
P. SOMPS CO. S. F. (Acid etched on shoulder) SODA WATER
GOLDEN WEST/ SODA WORKS/ SAN FRANCISCO/ CAL.
HERCULES/ (Image of Hercules with wings)/ MINERAL WATER
LIBERTY SODA WORKS/ (Eagle image) D.W.V.S.F.
HYGEIA/ MINERAL WATER Co./ SAN FRANCISCO/ THIS BOTTLE NOT TO BE SOLD
LYTTON SPRINGS/ (Pelican imager) SWEET DRINKS/ P.M.H. Co./ SAN FRANCISCO/ C. H. B.
MAJESTIC COTTLING CO. S. F.
MANHATTAN MINERAL/ WATER CO./ S. F. CAL.
NATIONAL/ SODA WORKS/ S. F.
NEW CENTURY/ SODA WORKS/ SAN FRANCISCO
NEW CENTURY / SODA WORKS/ SAN FRANCISCO. CAL.
NEW CENTURY/ STEAM SODA WORKS/ SAN FRANCISCO
NEW LIBERTY / SODA W. Co./ TRADE (Liberty Head) MARK/ S. F.

NONPAREIL/ SODA WATER CO./ S. F.
PEERLESS/ GINGER ALE CO./ S. F.
PHILLIPS / SODA WATER / CO./ S. F.
POPULAR/ SODA WATER Co./ S. F.
PIONEER / SODA WORKS/ TRADE (Shield with W) MARK/ S. F.
PIONEER / (Bear/ SODA WATER CO./ S. F.
C. A. REINERS & CO./ 723 TURK ST./ S. F.
G. ROTTANZI/ 23RD & BRYANT Sts. / S. F.
STANDARD/ SODA WORKS/ A/ C M/ M/ S.F.
ROYAL/ SODA WATER WORKS/ INC./ S. F. CAL./THIS BOTTLE/ NOT TO BE SOLD
SAN FRANCISCO/ SODA WORKS

SAN JOSE   Page 151-154
SAN JOSE SODA WORKS/ JOHN BALZHAUSER/ PROP./ SAN JOSE, CAL.
C. F. RILEY / Eagle facing right/ SODA WATER
C. F. RILEY/ Eagle facing left/ SODA WATER
WILLIAMS BROS. / SAN JOSE/ CAL.
CALIFORNIA/ SODA WORKS/ SAN JOSE, CAL.
CALIFORNIA/ SODA WORKS/ SAN JOSE/ CAL.
PAUL JEENICKE/ SAN JOSE
GOLDEN WEST / SODA WORKS/ SAN JOSE/ CAL.

SAN LUIS OBISPO   Page 154-156
O. TULLERMANN'S / MINERAL WATRER/ WORKS/ S. L. O.
S. L. O./ SODA WATER/ S. CERIBELLI
S. L. O. / SODA WORKS/ A. ALBERT

SAN PEDRO   Page 156-157
SAN PEDRO SODA/ AND/ BOTTLING WORKS/ SAN PEDRO, CAL.
STANDARD BOTTLING WORKS/ T/ SAN PEDRO, CAL. / THIS BOTTLE NOT TO BE SOLD
SAN PEDRO WHOLESALE CO./ SAN PEDRO, CAL.

SAN RAFAEL   Page 158-160
BUFFALO/ BOTTLING/ WORKS/ B. B. W./ SAN RAFAEL/ CALA.
B. B. W. / SAN RAFAEL
M. PETERSEN/ MARIN/ SODA WORKS/ SAN RAFAL (Misspelt)
M. PETERSEN/ MARIN/ SODA WORKS/ SAN RAFAEL
MARTIN PETERSEN/ SAN RAFAEL/ CAL.
KLAMMER & MALZ/ SAN RAFAEL/ CAL.

SANTA ANA   Page 161-162
GRUMBACH & SCHUMAKER/ SANTA ANA/ CAL. (Schumacher misspelt)
GRUMBACH & SCHUMACHER/ SANTA ANA/ CAL.
G. W. WELLS/ W/ SANTA ANA

SANTA BARBARA   Page 163-164
SANTA BARBARA/ SODA WORKS/ SANTA BARBARA
SANTA BARBARA/ BOTTLING Co. / SANTA BARBARA, CAL.
SANTA BARBARA/ BOTTLING Co./ SANTA BARBARA, CAL. / A.G.W.L.

SANTA CRUZ   Page 165-169

E. & J. LODTMANN/ SANTA CRUZ Co./ CAL.
J. LODTMANN/ SANTA CRUZ Co. / CAL.
P. WESSELHOEFT/ SANTA CRUZ, Co. / CAL.
WESSELHOEFT/ SANTA CRUZ, Co. / CAL. (Slugged into some Lodtmann bottles)
SANTA CRUZ/ J. J. / SODA WORKS/ SANTA CRUZ/ CAL.
PACIFIC SODA WORKS/ R/ SANTA CRUZ
PACIFIC SODA WORKS/ P/ SANTA CRUZ
EAGLE (Eagle) SODA WATER / AND/ BOTTLING CO./SANTA CRUZ, CAL./ THIS BOTTLE NEVER SOLD
BITHER BRO./ SANTA CRUZ/ CAL.

SANTA MARIA — Page 170
F. BAUMAN/ SODA WORKS/ SANTA MARIA

SANTA MONICA — Page 170
SANTA MONICA/ BOTTLING/WORKS

SANTA ROSA — Page 171-177
T & H/ SONOMA / CAL.
T & Co. / SONOMA/ CAL.
P. J. S. & Co./ SONOMA/ CAL.
P. J. SULLIVAN/ SANTA ROSA/ CAL.
F. & J. / SANTA ROSA (On bottom)
HUDSON & PALMER /SANTA /ROSA/BOTTLING CO./ SANTA ROSA (Reverse 33)
HUDSON & PALMER /SANTA /ROSA/BOTTLING CO./ SANTA ROSA
SANTA ROSA BOTTLING CO./ SRBCo. / SANTA ROSA CAL. / REGISTERED
SANTA ROSA BOTTLING CO./ SRBCo. / SANTA ROSA CAL.
SANTA ROSA BOTTLING CO./ SRBCo. / SANTA ROSA CAL. (Reverse THIS BOTTLE IS NEVER SOLD)
PRIDE OF SANTA ROSA (Paper label)
I.X. L. / SODA WORKS/ STOLLAR BROS. / SANTA ROSA
GILT EDGE BOTTLING WORKS/ SANTA ROSA/ CAL./ BOTTLE IS NEVER SOLD

SAUSALITO — Page 177
MASON & Co./ SAUSALITO (Bottom 4 M's)

SELMA — Page 178
MORGAN & Co./ SELMA, CAL.

SISSON — Page 178
MT. SHASTA SODA WORKS/ SISSON, CAL.

SONOMA — Page 179
SONOMA VALLEY/ SODA WORKS/ SONOMA/ CAL.
S. V. S. W./ (acid etched on shoulder of Bay View bottling works, Seattle Washington bottle)

SONORA — Page 180-183
LEONARD / SONORA/ CAL.
THOMAS LEONARD / SONORA/ SODA WORKS/ SONORA, CAL.
M. TERZICH/ SONORA/ CAL.
M. TERZICH SONONA CAL. (around bottom of face)
SAMMONS SODA WORKS/ SONORA/ CAL.
BACON'S SODA WORKS/ SONORA, / CAL.
BACON'S SODA WORKS/ SONORA/ CAL. (no comma after Sonora)

ST. HELENA	Page 183-184

ST. HELENA/ SODA WORKS
ST. HELENA BOTTLING & COLD STORAGE CO. / GINGER ALE (Paper label)

STOCKTON	Page 184-187

NATIONAL SODA WORKS (Horseshoe on face)
B (Stands for Belding. No lines in B)
B (Stands for Belding. Lines in B)
B / STOCKTON

TRUCKEE	Page 187-188

C. THOMAS/ TRUCKEE/ CAL.
C. THOMAS/ TRUCKEE

TULARE	Page 188

TULARE/ SODA WORKS

UKIAH	Page 189-190

UKIAH SODA WORKS/ UKIAH/ CAL. (Large embossing)
UKIAH SODA WORKS/ UKIAH/ CAL. (Small embossing)
G. W. EPLER

VACAVILLE	Page 190

SOLANO/ SODA WORKS/ VACAVILLE/ CALIFORNIA

VALLEJO	Page 191-192

EMPIRE SODA WORKS/ VALLEJO, CAL.
EMPIRE SODA WORKS/ VALLEJO
W. TOMEY/ VALLEJO

VENTURA	Page 192

ACME/ SODA WORKS/ VENTURA/ CAL.

VISALIA	Page 193

VISALIA/ SODA/ WORKS

WATSONVILLE	Page 193-194

S/MARTINELLI/ WATSONVILLE
WATSONVILLE/ BOTTLING WORKS/ H. A. P. / PROPRIETOR
WATSONVILLE/ BOTTLING WORKS/ H. A. R. / PROPRIETOR (H.A.R. instead of H.A.P.)

WILLOWS	Page 195

WILLOWS/ BOTTLING WORKS/ WILLOWS, CAL.

WOODLAND	Page 195-197

WOODLAND SODA/ WORKS
C M B / WOODLAND
O. A. / WOODLAND

YREKA	Page 197-198

B. GILBERT/YREKA
MEAMBER BROS./ YREKA
MEAMBER BROS./ PINEAPPLE SODA/ YREKA, CAL. (Paper label)

MYSTERY BOTTLE	Page 199

www.ingramcontent.com/pod-product-compliance
Lightning Source LLC
Chambersburg PA
CBHW042357070526
44585CB00029B/2970